CONSTRUCTING
KNOWLEDGES

CONSTRUCTING KNOWLEDGES

The Politics of Theory-Building and Pedagogy in Composition

SIDNEY I. DOBRIN

State University of New York Press

Published by
State University of New York Press, Albany

© 1997 State University of New York

For information, address State University of New York Press,
State University Plaza, Albany, NY 12246

Production by David Ford
Marketing by Bernadette LaManna

Library of Congress Cataloging-in-Publication Data

Dobrin, Sidney I., 1967–
    Constructing knowledges : the politics of theory-building and
pedagogy in composition / by Sidney I. Dobrin.
        p.   cm.
    Includes bibliographical references.
    ISBN 0-7914-3343-9 (alk. paper). — ISBN 0-7914-3344-7 (alk.
paper : pbk.)
        1. English language—Rhetoric—Study and teaching—Theory, etc.
    2. English language—Composition and exercises—Study and teaching-
    -Theory, etc. I. Title.
    PE1404.D635 1997
    808'.042'07—dc20   96-21040
                                                                      CIP

10   9   8   7   6   5   4   3   2   1

*This one's for
Mom, Dad, Adam, and Ben.*

Never could there be more love.

CONTENTS

PREFACE

Writing a book like this involves all sorts of frustrations. I'm particularly frustrated by the confines of time while finishing this book. At the same time I'm putting finishing touches on this project, I'm also scrambling to write a paper on theory and practice for CCCC. Looking at the abstract I submitted, I realize that what I want to articulate in the paper has absolutely nothing to do with what I proposed to discuss over a year ago. I'm thinking about the same things but in different ways. My thoughts have been influenced by scholarship and experiences since I proposed the abstract, and what I want to say now isn't what I wanted to say then. The same is true for this book: there are things I want to add, to remove, to update with what others have said since I started writing over a year ago. But presses have deadlines, and I can't endlessly revise if I ever want to contribute this book to the Conversation. And what of the year that these pages drift about in the hands of editors and printers before they enter the Conversation? Will I want to have written this in other ways? Composition is a thing that is never done; writing, like painting, is a composition that may never be finished. Just as I may continually add paint, push the colors around on my canvas, redirect lines, redraw huge portions of the thing, I don't want the book to be through; I could add so much more color.

Yet, within this frustration, I find myself asking more crucial questions about the relationship between the very time that frustrates me and the activity of theorizing. There tends to be a sense of progressivism that surrounds conversations of theory and theorizing. The activity of theorizing which I support in these pages entails a notion that we move toward better knowledges as we theorize and speculate. That is to say, when we examine the activity of theoretical speculation in conjunction with time, theory gets swallowed up in the very metaphors by which we define time. Time and theory mirror each other; time and theory are progressive narratives. We even define time in terms of theory and particular paradigms of knowledge: postmodernity, the age of romanticism, the Renaissance. In contemporary paradigms, we begin to requestion the very construct of time (a subject about which I don't claim to be an expert). We acknowledge the ability to occupy multiple spaces, multiple sites. We reconceptualize the ability to occupy particular moments of time. Certainly, we occupy more than one theoretical position at a time; perhaps our thinking about what theory *is* must also move toward new metaphors—metaphors I'm not yet willing to suggest but new sites just the same. On the one hand, the ways in which we discuss the activity of theorizing suggest a progressive narrative and, on the other hand, theory building—the construction of totalizing narratives—looks to solidify knowledge in time. That is, time and theory seem to operate in an exchange medium, and there seems to be a need to reconceptualize the metaphors by which we define theory. But that is now only a frustration.

Even though the byline on the cover of this book identifies me as "author," this book, by no means, came into existence solely by my writing. I owe many thanks to those people who spent countless hours discussing, arguing, editing, critiquing, and analyzing the words and thoughts which are constructed here. I hope I have never been foolish enough to think this writing—that any writing—emanates from inside "me"; I see it is a product of collaboration, discussion, social interaction, and a willingness to allow for knowledge to be influenced—controlled—by social, cultural, economic, ideological forces beyond my control. Having said that, I wish to sincerely thank those people whose influence and guidance have helped shape this book: First and foremost my thanks to Gary A. Olson for his incredibly detailed comments on just about every sentence offered in these pages and for his patience and friendship. And thanks to Patricia Bizzell for her willingness to read and critique drafts at various stages of writing and for guiding me toward more dynamic ways of thinking about rhetoric and composition. In addition to Pat's and Gary's extensive help, Tom Kent and Susan Miller have been—and continue to be—incredibly influential in how I come to particular concepts and ideas, and I thank them for their comments on this work. Let me offer broad thanks to all of those who had any influence on the writing of this book: Evelyn Ashton-Jones, Marilyn Minor, Jeff Karon, Lynda Haas, Priscilla Ross and SUNY Press, and the anonymous manuscript reviewers. Finally, I offer my deepest thanks and respect for the communal work ethic and never-ending friendship of a group of compositionists affectionately known as the "idyots": Raul Sanchez, Irene Ward, Tom West, Todd Taylor, Steve Brown, and Julie Drew.

FOREWORD

PATRICIA BIZZELL

Constructing Knowledges provides us with a thorough and timely analysis of attacks on theory in composition studies, both past and present. As Dobrin points out, theoretical implications have traditionally been denied to the teaching of writing, reflective of the sense within the parent field of English studies that this work is necessarily simplistic in method and impoverished in content. Moreover, writing teachers have traditionally responded to this denigration by defiantly embracing it—ever a tactic of the oppressed—and announcing their pride in their preoccupation with pedagogy. Now, to this traditional dissociation of theory and practice in composition studies is added the deconstruction of theory making itself as a metacognitive activity by critics such as Stanley Fish, a view that has been influential among teachers of writing.

Dobrin shows us that any declarations of the death of theory are not only premature but counterproductive. He helps us to see that the teaching of writing needs to be informed by theory—but also that the usefulness of this relationship depends on what kind of theory we mean. When literary scholars denied theoretical import to composition, perhaps what they meant to convey was that the kind of theory that interested them—e.g., poetic theory—could not be developed with the use of examples from supposedly inept student writing.

This was not to say that composition could not have theory but just that whatever theory it might have would not be interesting to literary scholars.

In response to this denigration, writing teachers made a stronger anti-theory claim, implying not just that the preferred literary theories could not apply to their work but that all theories were useless jargons with little or no connection to pedagogy or any other real work in the world. This patently anti-intellectual stance—although, as Dobrin implies, it is still with us—began to meet opposition within the field as composition studies gained in status in the academy. Composition scholars began to try to devise theories that would apply to their work even if these would not be theories of interest to literary scholars.

These early developments of theory in composition studies, however, were still governed by the definition of theory that Fish and other postmoderns have attacked. This is what Dobrin calls "Theory" with a capital T—that is, theory as a set of lawlike generalizations that predict the behavior of specific instances with precision. This is the kind of theory that is associated with modern science. In our zeal to enhance the intellectual credibility of our discipline, we may once have hoped to be able to describe the composing process in the same way that scientific theory describes a chemical process.

But sciencelike theory in composition studies met with criticism from people who subscribed to the postmodern view that human rationality cannot operate in a pure form, as it must do to generate this kind of theory. In this view, lawlike "Theory" with a capital T cannot exist. Rather, the postmodern critics argue that human thinking is always influenced by personal, social, and historical circumstances, And as they bear upon language use, these circumstances, not putative "laws" of composition, are what composition scholars should be studying.

Because we reject ill-applied or jargon-filled theories, because we do not believe in the possibility of lawlike theories does not mean that all forms of theory must be rejected. In place of "Theory," we can have "theory" with a small t, as Dobrin puts it. Whereas "Theory" tends to be thought of as something static, like a table of laws, "theory" is better thought of as a process or an activity—"theorizing" or "theory talk." Theorizing does not claim to generate laws or predict instances with invariant rigidity; indeed, it presents itself as provisional, thus avoiding the strictures that postmodern critics place on "Theory."

But that is not to say that theorizing is not useful. Theorizing might be defined as thinking about what one is doing—reflecting on practice—but thinking about it in a systematic way, trying to take as much as possible into account, and using the ideas of other thinkers wherever they may be helpful. Theorizing might then lead not to laws but to rules of thumb, which enable us not to predict outcomes infallibly but at least to speculate about which are more or less probable. Unlike "Theory," theorizing will not dictate practice, but it may guide it. This is the kind of theory most useful for composition studies in Dobrin's analysis.

This kind of theory—theorizing—is defended even by educators as devoted to urgent practical teaching problems as Paulo Freire. The example of his life committed to helping oppressed people all over the world should help to give credit to theorizing and save it from the charge of being a mere sterile game, in case any teachers of writing are still concerned about this danger of theory. In fact, in *Pedagogy of the City*, Freire emphasizes the need for a relationship between theory and practice in his work, saying, "The practice of thinking about practice deprived of a serious and well-founded theoretical tool would result in a sterile and boring game" (104).

Note that Freire suggests here that theorizing, while it may be seen as a "practice" on the same logical level as the practice of pedagogy, is more than simply "thinking about practice." Some sort of "theoretical tool" is required as well, which may be what I have attempted to characterize above as additional obligations to be systematic and to take other thinkers' ideas into account. Furthermore, theorizing must be "well-founded," attempting to give good reasons and make persuasive arguments, and it must be "serious"—that is, as we may infer from Freire's career, aimed ultimately at fostering projects for the common good.

These elements of theorizing emerge more clearly in the anecdote Freire uses as an illustration in this passage. He recalls a time when he was asked to consult with a literacy team working with the poor in São Paulo. The team were concerned that their evaluation meetings with radical community leaders had become stalled; as they put it, "The problems are always the same and we never speak about solutions, about strategies" (104). Freire diagnoses the problem this way:

> What was taking place was, up to a certain point, that the group leadership did not have sufficient theoretical knowledge to, in the process of thinking about the practice of the people involved, unveil with them the obstacles and their raison d'etre. All of a sudden, the leadership began to feel

lost. In reality, the leadership lacked the theoretical tools to help it illuminate the practice about which the militants were attempting to think, but were unable to do so. (104–5)

Freire concludes this passage with a list of no less than nine—"to name a few," as he says—theorists with whom an educator must be acquainted before attempting to devise productive practice.

The point here, I take it, is that theorizing could have directed these educators more quickly down a productive path toward new approaches. Theorizing could have helped them to see more quickly what solutions would more probably help them get out of their difficulties. Instead of trying every key on the bunch, doggedly, one after the other, they could have gone first to those that looked most like they would fit the lock. And they would then have been able to move forward more quickly with a specific project to promote social justice by fostering literacy in this community.

If Freire is right, then Dobrin's study is, indeed, timely. Dobrin's investigation of the relationship between a number of currently prominent theories in composition studies and the practices they inform will help to renew our sense of the value of theorizing to generate useful new practice. Furthermore, and importantly, Dobrin's study helps us to see the value of theorizing even when it does not immediately lead to new solutions in specific practical situations. We cannot always know what we are going to get from theorizing, and we cannot restrict our freedom of inquiry with a requirement that the pedagogical benefits must be demonstrated in advance. Dobrin helps us to see theory as neither master nor servant but rather as colleague—one of those supremely helpful colleagues with whom frequent dialogue enhances our teaching and our thinking, with whom we can better enjoy the pleasures and rewards of reflection.

1

COMPOSITION AND THE POLITICS OF THEORY BUILDING

"I am not interested in choosing between balance and
tensions."
—*Gayatri Chakravorty Spivak,*
"Rhetoric and Cultural Explanation:
A Discussion with Gayatri Chakravorty Spivak"

Since Aristotle, scholars in the sciences and the
humanities have held the epistemological assumption that theoretical knowledge is superior to knowledge deriving from praxis because
it is generalizable and therefore more universally useful. This traditionally accepted view of theory has been challenged by contemporary
scholars. Criticism coming from various sources, including the neo-
pragmatists and postmodernists, has argued that theory cannot be
assumed to answer local problems generally and universally, and current thinkers instead argue for what Clifford Geertz has labeled "local
knowledge." In other words, current debates about the role of theory
ask the question, What is useful knowledge? Within the academy, and
in composition studies in particular, this inquiry has begun to call
into question the "usefulness" of theoretical knowledge in various—
and often unproductive—ways.

Contemporary scholars as diverse as Richard Rorty, Stanley Fish,
Donald Schon, and Stephen Toulmin have argued that we need to
approach theory with a more pragmatic agenda. These and other
thinkers are adamant about the need to focus on local practice: Toulmin claims that "there is probably no legitimate role for theory"
(Olson, "Literary" 306), and Fish goes so far as to argue that theory
cannot serve as a foundation for practice. In his argument against
the usefulness of theory, Toulmin claims that the process of developing theories requires abstraction, and he posits that theories argue
away from real life and deny direct application to specific situations.
Likewise, Fish argues that it is not theory that perpetuates change but
action. Toulmin writes that despite the apparent attempt "not to

build new, more comprehensive systems of theory with universal and timeless relevance," we need "to limit the scope of even the best-framed theories" (qtd. in Olson "Literary" 305).

Yet proponents of theory still see a need to found practice on theory. Scholars such as Lee Odell and Peter Elbow bring this argument to composition studies and—in contrast to Fish, Toulmin, and others who argue against theory—have attempted to identify ways in which theory is useful knowledge and can influence practice. Elbow, C. H. Knoblauch, Lil Brannon, and others who see value in theory posit that taking a "theoretical stance" in determining practice benefits the execution of practice. Knoblauch and Brannon claim that a pedagogy's underlying philosophy (or the theory on which it is based) is extremely important in developing that pedagogy.

This debate has a direct impact on those of us in rhetoric and composition since our task as teachers and scholars seems to be twofold: to participate in a practice, our pedagogy; and to produce theory that explains the nature, function, and operation of written discourse. In other words, on a daily basis we are forced to participate in this argument, or at least to acknowledge how this debate affects the profession. There is a great need to examine the ways in which compositionists bridge the gaps between current composition theories and classroom practices because current composition theories are generated from a variety of ideological and epistemological backgrounds. Many competing theories have evolved along with discussions about how to use theory in developing successful composition pedagogies, and with this relatively new questioning of the role of theory and the importance of theoretical knowledge in mind, we need to examine the ways in which contemporary composition theory informs pedagogy: In what ways has theory been imported into the composition classroom? How has it succeeded or failed? *Should* theory inform pedagogy? Can it?

Four principal concerns must be considered in answering these questions: the ways in which current pedagogical scholarship incorporates or discredits current theory, the ways in which current theory accounts for—or doesn't account for—pedagogical needs, the ways in which the profession perceives the interaction between theory and pedagogy, and new ways in which compositionists can better use the tensions and balances between theory and practice to create pedagogies that will benefit students. I have quoted Gayatri Chakravorty Spivak in my epigraph as not being "interested in choosing between balance and tensions"; nor am I. I do not want to relieve the tensions created by a debate over the privileging of practice or theory, nor do I want to find balances in this debate, since these tensions and balances perpetuate continuing discussion and thought in the field. Instead, I want to try to better understand the ways in which tensions and balances between theory and practice are most beneficial. Patricia Bizzell argues that, while theory helps inform pedagogy, pedagogy must be indigenous—a recognition that both theory and practice are important in rhetoric and composition. It is this sort of *connection* I wish to explore.

WHAT IS THEORY?

For centuries, scholars have searched for ways to explain how aspects of both the physical and metaphysical worlds work. The search for universal explanations, or "truths," about how the world generally operates derives from a tradition of empiricism and inductive reasoning. In order to explain how things work, scholars have traditionally observed phenomena and translated these observations into universal explanations. In other words, there has been an attempt to explain how a category of things operates by observing a representative number of those things and then drawing conclusions about how all such things must necessarily operate. Such generalizable explanations depend on experience, observation, speculation, and analysis. Essentially, this activity of attempting to describe how certain phenomena work *in general* and therefore to predict how they will work in the future is what has become known as theorizing or theory building.

Etymologically, *theory* is derived from the Latin *theoria* and the Greek *theros*, both of which refer to the "spectator," which is closely related to "speculation" and to "speculum." *Theory* is also derived from or related to *theasthai*, "to observe or view," and *theōrein*, "to consider." The word itself suggests an empirical grounding: that a theory is derived from direct observation. Thus, someone who theorizes is a kind of "spectator," closely "observing" some reality and "mirroring" (as a speculum, or mirror, does) the observed phenomenon in precise descriptions of its nature. The theorist then "considers" or "speculates" on the nature of the phenomenon in order to arrive at generalizable statements, or universal truths, about how all members of the class to which the observed phenomenon belongs work. By reasoning that there are general characteristics and an identifiable true nature of like things, theory presupposes that the conclusions based on empirical observation and speculation must hold true in all cases of that phenomenon. For example, Aristotle, who is often credited as being the first botanist, observed various plants, noted their characteristics, compared and contrasted them with other plants, and arrived at general conclusions as to which plants belong to which families, what conditions certain plants need in order to thrive, when certain plants would blossom, and so on. Or, as one of the great early theorists of poetics, Aristotle observed the drama of his time, noted characteristics of successful and less successful drama, speculated about what made good drama work (as in his discussion of *catharsis*), and thus derived his theory of poetics. In short, theory is the inference of how all like things operate based on repeated instances of observation, speculation about those observations, and the construction of accurate explanations of what the phenomenon in question is and how it works.

Theory is often contrasted with law, as in "a law of physics." Occasionally, but very rarely, what begins as a theory reaches the status of law—that which has been verified beyond any doubt. It is this high degree of certainty that characterizes a law. So, for example, given the law of gravity, we can be reasonably certain that an apple rolling off the edge of a table will always plummet to the ground below and will do so at a rate of velocity relative to its weight and mass. In a certain sense, theories strive to be but can never quite attain the status of law. Whether explicitly or not, the act of theorizing is an attempt to move toward the certainty of a law, constantly refining and adjusting a theory's "truth value" in an attempt to approach ever greater degrees of certainty in its explanation of phenomena. While a law is often a tacit goal of theory, theory, for the most part, cannot reach that level of confirmation since most theories cannot (with the possible exception of some aspects of physical reality) be tested to the extent of absolute verification. Of course, postmodern theory has put into question even the once sacrosanct absolute reliability of laws. For instance, a law of physics stipulates that water always boils at 212 degrees Fahrenheit; however, the boiling point of water is also dependent upon other variables, such as altitude. Context must always be considered. So even physical laws may not always operate with the kind of absolute certainty once thought.

Although theorizing is an attempt to arrive at accurate explanations of some phenomenon, theories are not necessarily rigid, didactic, or even stable. In fact, most often theory is organic, receptive to new observations, additional facts, further speculation. Theory accounts for experience and allows new experience to alter or contribute to the evolution of that theory. Theory provides a framework within which one can operate, ask questions, even alter or refine principles of that theory based on new experience, new observation. That is, theory does not allow itself to stagnate; it pushes and pulls its way to understanding how a set of phenomena, a field, a body of knowledge, operates. Because of their evolutionary quality, theories are not usually seen in terms of *true* or *false*; rather, new theories are seen as more adequate or more useful explanations of phenomena for which past theories could not account. Theory leaves room for revision; universal explanations can be rethought. Thus, the real value of theory has been its evolutionary, generative power, its ability to adapt and change over time in the light of further speculation. And, of course, theorizing can be at times a subversive or revolutionary force, overturning previous assumptions or theories.

Ever since the ancient Greeks, theory has been considered a superior form of knowledge to that deriving from local practice. *Theoria* and *praxis* have most frequently been placed in binary opposition, with *theoria* serving as the privileged term, despite various attempts to argue that the two are always in some dialectical (not hierarchical) relationship. That is, despite the fact that Aristotle and other thinkers since have occasionally acknowledged that theory and practice can and should inform one another, the actual intellectual politics has been such that theoretical knowledge has always been privileged. Because theory is perceived to have explanatory power well beyond any local or particular instance or situation, it has been deemed more generally useful than knowledge deriving solely from local practice. This assumption can be seen most concretely in the academy's privileging of scholarship or research over teaching. Thus, we find in the academy in general and composition in particular that theory is pitted against practice, as though one could exist in some pure form without the other. Despite arguments to the contrary, however, even if we wanted to, we cannot force theory and practice into binary opposition: this is theory; this is practice. The two are so bound up, intertwined, enmeshed in one another—to the point of actually depending on the other, or of even becoming the same thing—that we cannot actually discern between the two at points.

Practice cannot be separated from theory. And yet we can talk about theory for theory's sake but not practice for practice's sake. Why? Because practice cannot exist without theory. Practice (particularly classroom practice) evolves from some theory, whether consciously or tacitly. Even the most inexperienced teachers who may be completely unaware of the origins of their practice use a pedagogy that was founded in some theory. For instance, many beginning teachers come to a classroom and operate based on a model that they enjoyed as a student or that was professed to them by a more experienced practitioner. This practice still originates in some theoretical standpoint. Practice is not produced through some form of immaculate conception; it is derived, in one fashion or another, from theoretical roots. And while beginners or "amateurs" may operate tacitly from some theoretical perspective, most "professionals" operate consciously from some theory; they recognize that some theory contains the basic assumptions under which they have chosen to operate.

Despite the debates over whether theoretical or practical knowledge is more useful and over whether the two can even really be separated, what *is* generally agreed is that theory has the potential to usefully inform pedagogy. Theory allows itself to influence, to inform how practice operates; it encourages general, universal explanations for how phenomena occur in the classroom, but it does not necessarily answer specific, local problems. Arguing about *the* precise role of theory in composition has become an important and at times polarizing debate. Before addressing this debate, however, it is necessary to explore how various postmodern theorists have problematized the very nature of theory and even questioned whether in fact theory *qua* theory exists.

BIG *T*s AND LITTLE *T*s

Since theorizing has been a major part of traditional knowledge-making processes, critiquing how we use and produce theory has become prominent in intellectual discourse. In the traditional view of theory that I have described, all theory attempts to provide explanations that are always true everywhere; that is, theory aspires to the condition of law. This tradition might recognize that there are areas in which the theory-governed behavior might be variable, or less lawlike. Also, this tradition might recognize that rhetoric enters while theories are being developed, tested, and spread, but that kind of theory-talk ceases once the theory becomes established, becomes lawlike.

A Cliff's Notes version of Western intellectual history might say that modernism takes this traditional view of theory to an extreme by attempting to bring everything under the rule of science. Scientific theory becomes paradigmatic theory in modernism, and scientific theory claims to subsume (or claims soon to subsume) everything humans can experience or know. This overly-summarized version might then go on to say that postmodenism calls these claims of scientific theory into question. Postmodernism attacks the traditional view of theory at the root by denying that human rationality can operate in a pure form, but in the traditional view, human rationality must so operate in order to generate theory. Rather, postmodernism claims that human thinking is always influenced by personal, social, and historical circumstances. Thus, there can be no "rationality" of the kind on which the tradition—and modernism a fortiori—based its claims to scientific hegemony.

One of the core arguments made against theory comes from the postmodern position that contends that a move toward generalizable, universal systems of explanation is an Enlightenment rationality maneuver; it is an attempt to erect a foundation of truth through rational processes. Generalized theory establishes a type of grand narrative that cannot really exist; it is only an illusion, and this is why we have many exceptions to various theories. Scholars like Rorty, Fish, and Toulmin attack theory, the real essence of what theory is supposed to do. This argument revolves around, as Toulmin and Rorty suggest, distinguishing between *theory* with a small *t* and *Theory* with a big *T*. They argue that *Theory*—universal, generalizable, grand explanations—cannot reliably answer local problems even while the activity of theoretical speculation itself may be useful, though in a limited way.

The postmodern critique of theory argues that it has no place in postmodern discourse. Or as Toulmin puts it, "There is probably no legitimate role for theory with a big *T*; we should be prepared to kiss rationalism goodbye and walk off in the opposite direction with joy in our hearts" (306). Unfortunately, given the way this debate is presented, this position (as held by Rorty, Toulmin, and Fish, in particular) frequently appears to posit the activity of theorizing (as opposed to theory building) as misguided. This is not what these scholars actually mean, though they are often interpreted as arguing so.

It is clear that the postmodern critique of theory stems from the idea that the foundational project from the Aristotelians on, particularly that of Enlightenment rationality, has been an attempt to establish kinds of "almost-law" explanations for phenomena, natural or metaphysical. According to the anti-theory position, this tendency to look for grandiose explanations is misguided for multiple reasons. This camp argues that it is impossible to devise a satisfying, generalizable universal answer that actually explains all facets of a phenomenon because particulars will always dictate. In other words, theory building, according to the postmodern critique, is simply another aspect of essentializing, of trying to grab hold of the essences of things, of trying to find stable truths, of trying to offer universal solutions. Scholars who adopt this line of thinking argue against the prototypical Enlightenment move: that once one has theorized about a lamp, for instance, one can derive explanations about how all lamps operate. This argument makes sense in the postmodern critique in that it perceives theorizing as necessarily another way of creating a type of grand narrative. In a postmodern world, we recognize that the urge to fashion totalizing narratives is misguided. But it ought to be said that these thinkers do not argue that the whole activity of theorizing—that is, engaging in some sort of hermeneutic speculation—is meaningless. If this were their position, their arguments would be hypocritical, since they too are engaged in theorizing even while they denounce theory building.

While the postmodern critique of theory is certainly correct in its criticism of the attempt to create master narratives through theory, Fish, Toulmin, and others perhaps dismiss theory too readily as having *no* impact on practice. Earlier, I mentioned Bizzell's argument that theory does inform classroom practice while classroom practice must also be indigenous. It is this connection between *Theory* and *theory* that is most beneficial in considering the role of theory in composition studies or in intellectual endeavors generally. Theory, and theoretical speculation, must be pursued more thoroughly in order to find connections between *Theory* and *theory*. The search for ways in which theoretical speculation informs local practice must be pursued from both theoretical and practical angles in order for such pursuits to be beneficial.

ANTI-FOUNDATIONALISM
AND THEORY FEAR

Anti-theoretical stances deriving not from the postmodern critique but from a conservative perspective often assume that in order for theory to be of use it must lead to relevant practice; theory for theory's sake, according to the anti-theory position, is useless. Though perhaps misguided, this complaint is at least understandable, but what is equally bound up in the anti-theory position, though not as immediately obvious, is a fear of the ways in which contemporary theory sees the world. I am speaking particularly of theories that have been labeled by Fish and others as "anti-foundational." This term refers to current theory that, as Ruth E. Ray puts it,

> denies the existence of universal truths, claiming that all inquiry, all findings, all "truths" are inseparable from the historical, political, and cultural contingencies that produce them. In short, all knowledge is "socially constructed," and the inquiring self is always "situated" within a belief system, whether one realizes it or not. (11–12)

Or as James C. Raymond sees it:

> What is most frightening [about theory] is its antifoundationalism. No one can alleviate that fright in those who feel it; relativism, antifoundationalism, postmodernism—all facets of the same phenomenon—do, in fact, threaten assumptions many people think they need to make sense of their lives. (91)

In other words, anti-foundationalist theories reject absolute standards by which truth can be found, since, as Patricia Bizzell puts it, "the individual mind can never transcend personal emotions, social circumstances, and historical conditions" (*Academic* 204). The notion of an ungrounded truth that anti-foundationalism suggests is a difficult idea for many to accept, particularly for those who want to ground theory in accountable, recognizable, stable practices. Because anti-foundationalism seems to cast theoretical and intellectual pursuits into a chaotic relativism in which nothing can be specified with certainty, many on the anti-theory side of the debate stand against theoretical advancement of this sort in fear of what these theories suggest about both the world and how we teach. "There is, on the one hand," Raymond tells us, "a denial of theory or a profound anxiety that it will result in a bottomless relativism, a chasm yawning into nihilism and despair" (87). Because anti-foundationalist theory shakes the very ground of the Western tradition and thereby seems, at least at first, counterintuitive, it should be no surprise that it frightens people; we have all invested much in the myths of "progress" and truth building, and now they are slipping away. It becomes easier to argue that such theoretical lines do not serve any positive goal and are, in fact, counterproductive to established ways of thinking than it is to engage these theories in more productive ways.

Ultimately, as I have suggested, this conversation revolves around knowledge making: How does theory inform practice? Does it? Should it? Is practical knowledge or theoretical knowledged privileged? All of these are issues that are of great concern to compositionists. While some compositionists operate from within the field to voice their concerns about theoretical pursuit, the theory debate has not been limited to composition or even to the academy. In fact, this debate has become a crucial issue to the academy as a whole, both in terms of how the academy engages knowledge making—what is useful knowledge?—and in terms of how the outside world perceives the academy.

ANTI-THEORY FROM WITHOUT

The issue of theory/anti-theory is one of epistemology, meaning making—a matter as important to the rest of the academy as to our small field. The theory/anti-theory debates have been voiced in numerous contexts through various media. We read or hear of other departments, entire universities, and even individuals and groups outside of the academy damning academics for ignoring what appear to be obvious practical problems in the classroom—for example, why our students are not as literate as they should be—and for pursuing theoretical enterprises that do not help solve "real" issues of education.

The problem of how the intellectual world is perceived has been noted by many, particularly by those who locate themselves in the anti-theory camp. Maxine Hairston writes, "I'm also very concerned about the image of the profession I think the magazine [*College English*] would convey to the public if they read it (thank goodness they don't!): that of low-risk Marxists who write very badly, and are politically naive, and seem more concerned about converting their students from capitalism than in helping them to enjoy writing and reading" ("Comment" 696). Hairston, though incorrect in her assessment of theory production, as I will discuss in a moment, has reason to be concerned. On any given day, in just about any mass media forum, one can find sentiments of anti-intellectualism and condemnations that academics are not doing their jobs—educating students—but are wasting time and taxpayers' money studying useless topics for no apparent reason. Take for instance Bill Watterson's "Calvin and Hobbes" comic strip from February 11, 1993. In this strip, Calvin (a hyperactive five-year-old with the vocabulary of an intellectual) comments (in three frames), "I used to hate writing assignments, but now I enjoy them. I realized that the purpose of writing is to inflate weak ideas, obscure poor reasoning, and inhibit clarity. With a little practice, writing can be an intimidating and impenetrable fog! Want to see my book report?" Hobbes (the real brains of the duo) reads Calvin's paper title, which sounds curiously evocative of any number of papers presented at the MLA convention: "The Dynamics of Interbeing and Monological Imperatives in *Dick and Jane*: A Study in Psychic Transrelational Gender Modes." Calvin smugly adds, "Academia, here I come." The sentiment is obvious. What makes this particular display of anti-intellectualism interesting is that readers who are familiar with Watterson's daily strip recognize that he is keenly aware of current trends in the academy; he makes reference to feminism, postmodernism, and various other contemporary academic movements. This particular strip, while targeting academic writing, conveys a general feeling from outside of the academy that academics are hiding behind an "intimidating and impenetrable fog" of jargon used to "inflate weak ideas, obscure poor reasoning, and inhibit clarity." This sentiment is not limited to the funny pages, but it is particularly telling that the subject has found its way there.

Many spokespersons of the conservative right also have taken opportunities to create an anti-intellectual spirit through mass media. MLA bashing, as you well know, has almost become an annual sport. Columnist George Will, for instance, is particularly aggressive toward English departments and their engagements in theoretical pursuits. In one column he writes, "It might seem odd, even quixotic, that today's tenured radicals have congregated in literature [English] departments, where the practical consequences of theory are obscure. Obscure, but not negligible" ("Literary" 72). More recently, Will specifically targets writing programs as particularly negligent and the place where "The smugly self-absorbed professoriate that perpetrates all this academic malpractice is often tenured and always comfortable" ("Trendy"). Like most critics outside the academy, Will sees theory as needing to lead to practical, accountable application.

One can easily find similar attacks in various media and conversations just about every day. For instance, on a recent fishing trip, I spoke with a retired Air Force officer about the decline in fish on the beaches near Cape Canaveral. We had both heard of the large amounts of sand that had been dumped there to curtail beach erosion, and we were both aware of the damage this dumping had caused on the grassy bottom just off the beach. The officer assessed blame for the disaster this way: "The problem is that a bunch of college boys sat around theorizing about how to solve one problem without thinking about other problems. They needed to get out here and see what was going on. Seems that's what's been wrong with colleges these days—too much theorizing, not enough seeing how things really work." Even during this brief vacation from academic journals and conferences, I had found my way back into the crux of the theory/anti-theory debate. It is precisely from this misunderstanding of theoretical pursuit that the anti-theoretical stance grows. Those who find no use for "off-the-wall" theories argue that unless theory directly influences the ways in which our students learn, unless it leads to practice, it is merely a "far-out" way for scholars to waste time and money while leading relaxed lives in which the day's tedium seems to consist of pondering universal silliness.

ANTI-INTELLECTUALISM AND THE BATTLE WITHIN

This attack on the "activity of theorizing," arguing that theorizing is an activity people engage in as a kind of clouded state of thinking that is not in touch with reality, has also found its way into rhetoric and composition. Generalizations, this argument suggests, are too close to abstractions. Because this debate is perpetuated by the sentiment that intellectual theoretical pursuit promotes unclear, abstract, useless theory, the anti-theoretical stance in this debate becomes one of anti-intellectualism. This anti-intellectual position grows from the misunderstanding of theorizing as an activity, and it stands against the jargon, careerism, and clouded thinking that this position believes theorizing promotes. As Raymond puts it, "What's most disagreeable about theory is its jargon" (91).

I do not want to give a genealogy of how theory as a mode of inquiry or a knowledge-making tool has progressed in composition; this has been done often enough (see Ray or North, for example). I am more concerned with articulating how theory is viewed both within and outside of composition. Not only has theory taken on a significant role in composition, but also it has come to fore in larger debates over the role of the university in society as growing disdain for theory is becoming a crucial component in the creeping anti-intellectualism that now surrounds discussions of the academy. Within composition, the question of which sorts of knowledge to privilege over others has become a conversation that is central to the development of the field's identity as well as to that of the academy as a whole. In his 1991 plenary address to the Research Network of the Conference on College Composition and Communication, Gary A. Olson stressed to the community of compositionists the dangerous level to which this debate has evolved:

> More than any debate over which modes of scholarly inquiry are most valuable, or which journals privilege which mode, the theory/anti-theory split emerging in the field threatens to polarize us in unproductive ways—in ways that serve to silence debate and to narrow our conception of the discipline of rhetoric and composition. ("Role" 4)

Normally, I would disagree with Olson's concern over this debate; after all, such discussions over other modes of scholarly inquiry have propelled us into our current, shifting identities. In other words, such conversations generally have been a productive method by which we have shaped our evolving discipline. However, unlike previous debates this particular conversation has turned ugly and, thus, counterproductive.

Recently, our journals, monographs, books, conferences, and other scholarly forums have seen an explosive increase in the amount and quality of theoretical scholarship. At the same time, there has been a tremendous retaliation against this theoretical outburst—not only from within the field but also from many outside rhetoric and composition and even from some outside of the academy.

Within the field, this debate was most visibly manifested in a series of letters printed in the Comment and Response section of *College English*. Led by Hairston, past chair of the Conference on College Composition and Communication, several scholars voiced, in what were ultimately to become known as composition's "theory wars," a dissatisfaction with the theoretical road down which the field had been traveling. Hairston writes:

> I find the magazine [*College English*] dominated by name-dropping, unreadable, fashionably radical articles that I feel have little to do with the concerns of most college English teachers. . . . And do you think many readers of CE have the interest or patience to wade through such stuff? I don't. (695)

She continues:

> I hate to see the journal attempt to elevate its standing in English departments by publishing articles that are as opaque

and dull as anything in *PMLA* or *Critical Inquiry*. . . . I can't help but believe that most of us want clear, thoughtful articles on reading and writing theory and on teaching, not articles that are larded with the fashionable names and terms but which, in my opinion, seek more to serve the ambitions of the authors than the needs of the readers. (695–96)

Hairston is not alone in her concern. There are many examples from the Comment and Response section, but the following statement from Mary Margaret Sullivan is representative:

I agree with Maxine Hairston regarding the content and style of articles that appear in *College English*. . . . My students need to know how to read and write, to think clearly and communicate effectively so they can become productive members of society, which are the basic needs of all of our students. (477)

Steve Kogan also agrees with Hairston and writes that the kinds of theoretical scholarship being discussed are "nothing but the voices of vested academic interests and a kind of political-professional careerism" displaying "almost perverse pleasure" that avoids confronting "the problems of the classroom, or rather, an engagement that is so theoretical (or seemingly theoretical) as to bury reality in clouds of words" (474). Jean Shepard offers a particularly telling comment:

I know about the text, the signifier, and the role of the reader; I've learned about Derrida and Fish, but I really don't know why. The sun is shining today for the first time in about a week. The breeze is moving loose branches on the trees outside my window; and I can't see why anyone cares about all of this terminology. Do the people who write these articles even have windows? (934)

Finally, Janet Hiller and Barbara Osburg bluntly assert that "no useful connection exists between composition theory . . . and the needs and practices of classroom teachers" (820).

Clearly, the sentiment seen in these and other of the Comment and Response letters, as well as in other forums, displays the anti-theory position: one that sees theorizing as an act designed to shut people out of a discourse, to promote careerism, and to engage in (perhaps, intentionally) clouded thinking. Of course, these and the other anti-theory positions that began to emanate from within the field have not gone unanswered. John Trimbur finds in Hairston's argument a recognition of why the field has taken this turn, and though he does not explicitly defend or privilege theory, he does recognize a key issue in why this debate has evolved as it has:

> It all depends on what you're interested in and how you align yourself in the current debates and projects within composition studies. . . . The fact of the matter—and what I think is really annoying Maxine—is that the intellectual context of composition studies has changed over the past five or ten years as teachers, theorists, researchers, and program administrators have found useful some of the ideas and insight contained in contemporary critical theory, whether feminist, poststructuralist, neopragmatist, or neomarxist. . . . The "mainstream" Maxine refers to isn't quite there anymore, at least not in the sense it was in the mid seventies. . . . Some teachers, and I would include myself, do indeed want to do more than help students "enjoy writing and reading." I see writing and reading as powerful tools for students to gain greater control over their lives and to add their voices to the ongoing debate about our communal purposes. (699–700)

Here Trimbur identifies a crucial issue: the changing mainstream. In order for rhetoric and composition (or any field, for that matter) to evolve, debates concerning useful knowledge must proliferate. As I mentioned earlier, writing teachers are necessarily positioned in this debate: we must participate in our practice, and in one way or another, whether directly or not, we must engage theory. As Trimbur puts it, "It all depends on what you're interested in and how you align yourself in the current debates . . . and projects within compositional studies" (699–700). The inherent problem, though, is consensus. In order for this debate, unlike many others, to be productive, we must not reach consensus. This debate must not be resolved and necessarily must lead to further debate. This is where Olson's fear comes to the fore. The "theory war" letters are only a skirmish compared to what has become a decidedly anti-intellectual attack on theoretical pursuits from within and without the academy.

Obviously, for our concerns, the theory debate must have proponents on both (all?) sides in order to perpetuate dialogue. Some of the anti-theory stances posed in this dialogue come from established, recognized, and respected scholars who engage the debate and are eager to dismiss theory for the wrong reasons: careerism, clouded thinking, jargon, lack of connection to practice. I do not necessarily mean to imply that all of these positions are presented as "attacks" directly associated with the "debate"; instead, many scholars dismiss theory in fear of how it changes our view of composition. What is most counterproductive is that it is specifically this fear of the changing mainstream that causes many scholars to see the theory camp as dangerous and to participate in a lynch-mob anti-intellectualism. I'll draw on a slightly unusual source for my example: a book review essay.

In his review of Lester Faigley's award-winning *Fragments of Rationality: Postmodernity and the Subject of Composition*, David Bleich takes a decidedly anti-theoretical stance in his condemnation of Faigley's text. Bleich, voicing his concerns that Faigley's theorizing neglects practical application and ignores important classroom-related issues, pans the book as an unnecessary theoretical exercise. He writes:

> For me, however, this book is frustrating because it does not relate the conjunction of writing and postmodernism to the urgent needs of today's academy. While the book may be well enjoyed by those who have no problem with the jargon of today's literary theory, it was hard for me to detect in it concern with the issues of collectivity now affecting schools and classrooms across the country, or enough sympathy for the new populations of students that are about to become minorities in school and society. (291)

Bleich continues, "I think that if concern for practical collective issues doesn't appear in a serious treatise such as this, then something is wrong with academic ways" (291). Here Bleich vocalizes an overriding concern of the anti-theory position: that theory is being produced that does not directly relate to practice. Because composition is seen by many as a solely service-oriented field, some scholars argue that theoretical inquiry must move toward practice in order to be of any use. In other words, much of the debate in composition concerning theory stems from the belief that all theory necessarily must somehow be tied directly to a practice in order to be useful. But scholarly endeavors pursued solely as theoretical inquiry are as necessary in continuing knowledge-making processes as theories that lead to practical application; that is, theory for theory's sake is or can be valuable. Within the field of composition, there are issues concerning written discourse or classical rhetoric, say, that have absolutely nothing to do with pedagogy. Yet such studies can provide valuable insights into the operations of written discourse or the relevance of classical rhetoric to contemporary concerns. If we define the field as solely service oriented, then, certainly, all theory in order to be useful must lead to helpful classroom practice. Rhetoric and composition, however, entails more than this limited definition. We, as scholars, are obligated to consider other aspects of written language if we are to move toward a fuller comprehension of composition and of written discourse in general. Making pedagogy a necessary end of theory places unneeded constraints or limitations on composition scholarship.

When Bleich attacks Faigley's theoretical pursuits, asserting that Faigley's work is "narrow, devoted mostly to theory, and not too much to the moments of human action and development," he speaks from the position that theory only has value when it exists as a means of deriving practical application (295). Bleich also contends, "It is clear that we teachers cannot wait for the revolution to teach us how to teach our students. So Faigley's solution of more theorizing, while plausible, is simply wrongheaded" (295). This critique illustrates a central assumption of the anti-theory position: that theory must inform praxis. This argument, coming from various sources in addition to Bleich, suggests that we curb intellectual theoretical pursuit that exists for reasons other than pedagogical development. But such sentiments do not go unchecked by other members of the composition community, though much of the anti-theoretical discourse that works its way into our conversations is blindly accepted. Bleich's attack comes in the form of a book review—a medium that generally serves as a terminal point in conversation in that it typically does not allow response or dialogue. However, the journal in which the review appears, *Journal of Advanced Composition*, claims as part of its policy to "promote a forum for scholars interested in all issues of 'theory'" (Olson, *On* v), and thus offered Raul Sanchez the opportunity to respond to Bleich's negative review.

In "David Bleich and the Politics of Anti-Intellectualism: A Response," Sanchez claims that Bleich's faulting of Faigley for excessive theorizing and lack of attention to practical issues fails to acknowledge the important role that theory plays in the continued development of composition. Sanchez writes, "This disdain for the theoretical and the political in composition, when mistaken for serious intellectual activity (as it was in Texas), drains our field of the insights it has accumulated over the last decade or so, insights that have made our discipline one of the most exciting and useful in the university" (579). Sanchez takes Bleich to task for what he sees as an oversimplification of the theory/anti-theory debate and a poorly thought out alliance with a hardline practice stance:

> Bleich seeks simple solutions to complex problems, prob-lems that do not lend themselves, if we mean to confront them honestly, to the kind of theory/practice distinction upon which he bases his critique. He believes that all this postmodern theory, with its fancy words and playful atti-tude, keeps us from discussing the "real" issues at hand. His frustration at Faigley's call for more theorizing is based on the assumption that theorizing itself is not a useful activity because we have enough of it already, as if we had topped off all the theory reservoirs as specified in our intellectual owner's manual. (580)

Sanchez continues:

> Theory and practice, if they are to inform each other mean-ingfully, must operate in a constant state of mutually transformative flux, and this is not the same as paralysis or aporia. Books like *Fragments of Rationality* help us begin to envision a future wherein such a relationship is possible. Reviews like Bleich's remind us of mistakes we have made in the past. (581)

Sanchez points to what he sees as the dangers Bleich and, by implication, others pose to rhetoric and composition's development. Arguments such as Bleich's are prolific in our conversations, and attacks like this do not benefit the field in ways that legitimate dis-cussions about the theory/practice or theory/anti-theory debate should. By taking the position that perceives theory as a vehicle for careerism, misuse of jargon, and misdirection of theoretical pursuit, Bleich, and others who argue similarly, force the debate about the role of theory to pursue a line of argument that must defend against these attacks. Conversation proliferates that essentially operates at a playground level: "Theory is bad." "Is not." "Is too."

Bleich's and other anti-intellectual, anti-theory proponents' posi-tions against theoretical pursuit are born from a misunderstanding of the use of theory and how the activity of theorizing operates. If, as

Bleich suggests, continued theorizing is "wrongheaded," then composition scholarship will stagnate, and composition as a field will be defined within the narrow confines of a service orientation. Bleich and others call for theory to directly influence their "real" classroom issues, but by dismissing theory—essentially calling for theory's stagnation—they opt for a static view of practice as well. If we are to cease our engagement with theory and its transformative nature, even the kinds of practical advancements the anti-theory/pro-practice camp calls for cannot be achieved.

Part of the anti-intellectual attack on theory derives from the sentiment that the discourse theorists use is seemingly out of touch with the discourse of "normal people." Bleich, for instance, comments that Faigley's book "may be well enjoyed by those who have no problem with the jargon of today's literary theory" (291). Certainly, this argument is correct in that people who participate in certain kinds of theorizing tend to have their own vocabulary, but is this necessarily a valid criticism? Jargon is the specialized vocabulary of a field, and the reason discourses take on a specialized vocabulary is so participants may communicate efficiently. If members of a discourse community know what is meant by a specific word, there is no need to define the concept each time it is discussed. Take the word *prewriting*, for example. Like other jargon, it carries with it a disciplinary understanding; there is no need to unravel all of the baggage associated with what *prewriting* entails when it is used within the discourse of composition. Jargon, in this sense, is beneficial, in that it allows compositionists to engage in conversations about the invention process efficiently. Granted, somebody who does not operate within the discourse, other than that he or she may intuit what the word means, may be mystified by its use, but the function of such language is not to appeal to the understanding of laypersons; it is to further discussions among members of a specific community.

Part of the problem that those who argue against theoretical language have with the activity of theorizing is that it seems gratuitously incomprehensible. Certainly, we can concede that certain theorists *might* be gratuitously incomprehensible, but it is not true that the entire notion of jargon, of specialized discourse, is designed to exclude people from a discourse. Jargon is a means by which discourse operates more efficiently, and that is what many who take this anti-theory position fail to comprehend. When outsiders encounter theoretical discourse, they often do not understand the jargon—"big words" such as *postmodern, antifoundational, poststructural, feminist*, and so on— and they become confused and frustrated, as Bleich does. Of course, this is a negative characteristic of jargon if a discourse is intended for a lay audience, but it is not a negative property if a discourse is directed at participants in that discourse. For example, the word *difference* is a word that resonates with multiple layers of meaning in postmodern discourse, and people who engage in postmodern discourse understand that it has many different tiers: gender difference, otherness, ethnic difference, systems of domination, and all the other connotations the word carries. Imagine what one would have to do if he or she were using that word and had to define its use in conversation. The amount of time and the number of sentences needed for such explanations would make the discourse unwieldy and inefficient. The argument against disciplinary language is ill conceived.

Theoretical language is frequently seen as a method that scholars use to make scholars appear more intelligent or to promote their personal careers—the careerism about which Hairston and others complain. No doubt there are people operating in any field who do this, and careerism exists in theory work. There is careerism everywhere—in the academy and without. However, it is unfair to allege that because a scholar works in theory that that scholar is necessarily a carreerist. It is a non sequitur to argue that because one engages in theory and uses theoretical language that one does so solely to get ahead in the world, and that is not the purpose of specialized vocabulary in theoretical discourses. Of course, these allegations make sense to a certain degree: perhaps, there are theorists whose scholarship we have to work at in order to comprehend; we may have to wonder, "Could this have been presented more clearly?" Yet, the move to dismiss theory on these grounds is not well founded; it is a dismissal based on misunderstanding. Thankfully, the study of the theory/practice interaction is being pursued in more formal, disciplinary, and responsible ways than some of my previous examples might suggest, as is the study of the resistance to theory.

THEORY, KNOWLEDGE MAKING, AND COMPOSITION

Though he doesn't pit practice against theory, Stephen M. North's taxonomy of participants in the field suggests varying contributions to the development of knowledge making in composition. This is central to the field's development: we need multiple modes of inquiry, multiple types of knowledge. Current thinking in composition recognizes that theory and practice are not self-contained. They not only rely on each other in transformative flux but also are dependent upon continued multimodal inquiry from various locations within the field in order to continually inform rhetoric and composition. In other words, whether privileged or not, both theory and practice must continue to evolve as hermeneutical systems of inquiry in composition; both have value. Recently, various scholars have employed local knowledge, experience, and context to call into question ways in which theory informs local practice—how we use theory and practice to create knowledge. The problem, in composition, Louise Whetherbee Phelps argues is that

> even as composition pursues this goal at one level of dis-
> course, a gap between theory and practice widens at another,
> like a fault line cracking the foundations of the discipline.
> Deep in the disciplinary unconscious runs a strong under-
> tow of anti-intellectual feeling that resists the dominance
> of theory in every institutional context of the field—jour-
> nals, conferences, writing classrooms, textbooks, teacher
> education—and even in some forms of theory itself. (*Com-
> position* 206)

Some scholars have tried to deal with these tensions. Phelps, for instance, draws on Gadamer to reach her goal of "constructing a new dynamic balance that reflects both theorists' purposes in seeking disciplinarity and teachers' intuitions about the proper role of knowledge in practical-moral activities" (*Composition* 206). Obviously, more than eight years later, Phelps's "new dynamic" balance has not occurred; nor should it, as I suggested by quoting Spivak earlier. However, Phelps's contribution to this conversation has helped in many ways to make sense of what role this debate plays in composition. She writes:

> A few thinkers in composition studies, Stephen North among
> them, are beginning to treat tensions between theory and
> practice as a philosophical dilemma for the field, and not
> simply a transitional phenomenon in a young discipline. In
> one interpretation, my own, teachers' continued hostility or
> indifference to composition theory offers a tacit critique of
> the utopian faith that formal knowledge can definitively
> guide human conduct, which has motivated the disciplinary
> project to study writing as a basis for teaching ("Toward a

Human Science"). Teachers are not merely afraid of "theory," or impatient with its abstractions and irrelevance; their intractability argues implicitly that practice is not an applied science, and they are not technicians. ("Practical" 863)

Certainly, Phelps is correct: the debate emerges from a young field attempting to establish its identity. It is a political, philosophical issue, an issue, as Trimbur points out, of where one stands. This becomes political and philosophical in that individual participants in the field must determine how the debate affects their participation—what knowledge they privilege. Ray goes so far as to suggest that those in the anti-theory camp "are reacting not to theory per se, but to the politics of theory—to a situation which promotes theory at the expense of practice, as seen in the experiential evidence they bring to bear" (21).

Within composition, the ties between theory and practice are at the center of our disciplinary conversation. Only recently have issues of anti-theory been taken to task as concerns in the theory/practice debate. Phelps contributes to this conversation a call for continued exploration of the relationship, the interaction, between theory and practice. She argues for a well-defined debate between theorists and practitioners. This is the sort of responsible conversation that allows theory and practice to interact in dialectical operation. The field will benefit by engaging in professional dialogue about the relationship of theory and practice.

The *debate* has become crucial for all scholars on all sides. The responsible position compositionists take in this debate is not one of moderator, not one of having answers, but of teachers and scholars who must participate in practice and who must engage that practice through theory. There is, then, a need to understand why pedagogy evolves as it does, a need to explore ways in which language operates. In composition, in other words, theory and practice each plays a significant role in our knowledge making; anti-theoretical arguments, when put forth in ways that do not contribute to our understanding of the theory/practice interaction, do not contribute beneficially to the field. By not engaging theory, we do not improve our pedagogy. As Pat Hinchey writes, "When the theoretical underpinnings of a practice are not clear—when the only rationale for a practice is that others say it 'works'—there are no clear guidelines to help implementers adapt a practice soundly to local conditions" (20).

Linda Brodkey writes that "despite seemingly indefinite variation in circumstances of teaching, composition teachers do not treat theory as a refuge from practice, but value instead what it can tell them about writing and writing pedagogy" (345). Her assessment of the value of theory is useful: theory can *tell* us more about writing and composition pedagogy. And yet some in composition deny the importance of theory and push for a focus toward practice.

Earlier I mentioned that ultimately this conversation falls to a matter of consensus—a consensus that ultimately must not be reached because consensus implies closure. John Schilb, in contrast, hints that an argument like this that does not reach consensus is destructive to scholarship in the field: "If we now argue over the priority of 'theory' and 'practice,' we do so partly because we've finally managed to wreck our own consensus on standards for scholarship" (95) Yet, to Schilb, and me, this debate is of crucial necessity for the field. Schilb recognizes the benefit such conversations offer to an emerging discipline:

> To deal with our apparent conflict between "theory" and "practice," then, I think we should encourage departments, conferences, and journals to sponsor forums that address the variety of disputes obscured by these terms. And the Idea would not be simply to acknowledge our different beliefs in a spirit of laissez-faire pluralism, but to juxtapose them for rigorous evaluation. I also think in such forums and in our individual work, we should deliberately undertake certain acts of displacement. (96)

As I have said, I am not attempting to solve the theory/practice, theory/anti-theory debates. Olson tells us that the "typical 'solution' or 'recommendation' to these struggles is that we place theory and practice in continual dialectical relationship, so that each may nourish the other" ("Role" 4). I agree wholeheartedly with this (non)solution, this strategy, and yet I disagree with Olson's claim that "attempts at balance are both reasonable and productive" ("Role" 4). We need tension as much as balance in order to perpetuate constructive conversation. Moreover, seeing this debate as simply an argument between theorists and practitioners is somewhat misleading. Olson argues:

> Seeing the issues in such narrow terms helps conceal some important tacit assumptions and draws our attention away from larger disciplinary issues we *must* address in future scholarship.
>
> Those who continually call for balance and who argue that theory must directly apply to practice have mistakenly

> constituted the discipline of rhetoric and composition as one
> in which the *raison d'etreis* is the teaching of writing: all
> research, all theory, all scholarship, in the field exists for the
> sole purpose of furthering and refining the *teaching* of com-
> position. ("Role" 4)

Compositionists who see the field in terms of a simple practice/theory binary in which practice must be privileged are misguided. Issues about discourse, language, and writing that exist beyond the classroom and that do not directly impact classroom practice must also be studied if we are to understand their operations. Theory does not necessarily have to inform pedagogy. The anti-intellectual positions that find theory useless unless it leads directly to classroom application deny a responsibility to the field. In Olson's words: "Theory for theory's sake is *not* an abdication of responsibility; it is *not* necessarily cynical careerism. Rhetoric and composition has become an intellectual discipline; we have an obligation to continue and even expand . . . theoretical scholarship" ("Role" 5). It is my belief that we must continue theorizing, continue our dialectic of theory and practice, keep debating, and stop doing so in unproductive, anti-intellectual ways.

2
POSTMODERNIST THOUGHT
AND THE TEACHING
OF WRITING

"What is a theory? What is a concept? What is a text?"
—*Michel Foucault*, Archaeology

"There are no Foucaultians."
—The Times, *London, June 27, 1984, 12*

"This writer writes to see what happens."
—*William A. Covino*, The Art of Wondering:
A Revisionist Return to the History of Rhetoric

Much of the backlash against theory in composition—
such as that discussed in Chapter One—is directed at postmodern
theory and its intervention into composition.[1] While scholars such
as Maxine Hairston and David Bleich caution the field against moving
in directions influenced by these contemporary theories, others such
as John Schilb, Patricia Harkin, Patricia Bizzell, James Berlin, William
Covino, and Bruce Herzberg have worked to bring postmodernism,
particularly poststructuralist theory, effectively into composition. The
postmodern agenda has seemingly become prominent in composition; it can be seen in the attempt to reevaluate, disrupt, and explore
language, to examine ways in which writing and writing practices
might be logocentric or phallogocentric. Postmodernism's various
incarnations raise important concerns about how the phenomena of
discourse and language operate.

Recently, some theorists in composition have challenged the field's
established theoretical paradigms. Many of these challenges have been
influenced by deconstruction and other postmodernist discourses. But
because these discourses have found their way into composition only
within the last few years, we have yet to determine exactly how their
insights might help to develop new pedagogies; nor have we reached
consensus as to what elements of these postmodernist discourses will be
most useful in our development of pedagogies. Nonetheless, postmodern

theory introduces important questions to composition, questions about power relations both in classrooms and throughout the various other communications that determine how we interact with the world. Or, as Lester Faigley puts it, "Postmodern theory offers an ongoing critique of discourses that pretend to contain truth and serve to justify practices of domination" (20). In other words, postmodern theory seeks to examine the traditional power structures that not only affect but also are perpetuated through language. Postmodern theories conceive, as Irene Ward writes, "truth and knowledge not as stable and determinable but as always contingent and dependent on local context. Knowledge, like language, can be understood, or have meaning, within *unique* communicative situations" (129). Or as Jack Blum writes:

> In claiming that knowledge must depend on language . . . and in maintaining that language is both sequestered from the real world and inherently self-subverting, poststructuralism not only shifts epistemology off the supposedly stable and self-evident foundations laid down in Cartesian philosophy but in doing so also precludes the possibility of establishing *any* epistemological foundation whatsoever: what we know is primarily conditioned by the assumptions and limitations of whatever "language game" we happen to find ourselves caught up in. (93)

This new epistemological perspective suggests that the postmodern composition pedagogies we construct might be profoundly different from their predecessors.

Several questions regarding the theory/practice debate come to the fore when reading scholarly work—such as James J. Sosnoski's "Postmodern Teachers in Their Postmodern Classrooms: Socrates Begone!" in *Contending with Words*—that addresses the role of postmodern theory in composition: Is theory in composition *really* a privileged knowledge as it has been in Western thought since the ancient Greeks? If so, why do compositionists seem eager to redirect theory to practice in nearly every instance? What is it about postmodern composition theory that makes it unique to composition? The contributing authors of *Contending with Words*, for instance, have produced powerful and useful scholarship in rhetoric and composition, both theory and practice, both in this text and elsewhere. When Sosnoski, in his summary response, attempts to tie all of these works together in a grand view of pedagogy, we have to begin to requestion exactly what kind of knowledge we are privileging. It is apparent that the university has traditionally privileged theory or research, but when we examine composition more closely, a field many regard as serving solely a service function, we have a different picture of knowledge. There is, as I've discussed, a great resistance to totalizing theory, to the act of theorizing, and even to those of us who wish to discuss theory. There is also a substantial attempt to bring theory and practice together, to balance them, to push the two toward organic, dialectical links, as *Contending with Words* does. Of course, what we do not hear as frequently is the call for the removal of practice from composition theory; we cannot hear this. In our continuing search for identity within the field, the overriding sentiment seems to be that without our practice we do not exist; we cannot exist solely as a research field. Hence, there is a general perception within the field that our theory must at all times inform practice and that postmodern theorizing in composition helps us achieve that goal by breaking down hegemonies that limit both theoretical and practical knowledge.

Since postmodern theories attempt to disrupt hegemonic, logocentric structures, these theories suit composition in that any form of critique, self-critique, deconstructive reading, and so on falls under its realm. Postmodern theory allows teachers to attempt to account for the diversity of students in varieties of pedagogies. In turn, then, the act of postmodern theorizing becomes less threatening to many as it potentially leads to a variety of approaches to composition instruction when it is *applied*. As Sosnoski puts it, "Writing is painful. Students hurt. Teachers hurt. Postmodern theorizing helps" (217). On the other hand, its free-moving, disruptive qualities also make it the most threatening of theories to some.

But why is it that over the past twenty years poststructuralism has developed at the same time composition studies has shed the most light on its own identity? Again, what is it about postmodern composition theory that makes it *composition* theory? Perhaps the contributors to *Contending with Words* offer the best clue (I discuss these works more thoroughly later in this chapter). In reading these essays and recognizing the desire to engage postmodern theory and practical needs of the contemporary, multicultural classroom, we see why composition has both embraced and rejected postmodernism and poststructuralism. Many compositionists believe that in order for the discipline to be legitimized composition needs a theory of its own—a theory that can potentially lead to practices that account for the diversities we encounter every day. Postmodern composition theory belongs to composition *because* of the ties that many insist must be made to our practice. Despite the agendas of many compositionists to free theory from practice and vice versa, many would argue that such separation cannot be accomplished in composition. There is a misunderstanding that in order for a theory to fall under the heading of "composition theory" it necessarily must engage composition—that is, the act of writing; it must engage a practice. This is not to say that theory needs a practice, but much of the field seems to believe that *composition* theory does. Certainly, Jacques Derrida, Michel Foucault, and others can offer theories that stand free of composition, but our desire to *apply* them suggests that many compositionists find value only in theories that can be applied to practice. We as a field are not willing to let a good theory go to waste; we look for application. And as I have said before, this is potentially a limiting characteristic of rhetoric and composition as a discipline because there are aspects of language about which we need to theorize and about which there are no necessary connections to pedagogy.

When we assess the value of a theory by its applicability (or lack thereof) to pedagogy, we are willingly accepting the role of service department in the university whether we like it or not. Of course, we must teach writing; ultimately, we cannot escape this role, though postmodernism and poststructuralism do allow us to introduce to our work various critical issues about writing, such as those discussed in this chapter. In our search for identity, we seem to have been forced into a paradoxical situation. On the one hand, the field of composition exists to serve the university—a subservient role away from which we have desperately been trying to move. On the other hand, by becoming "legitimized," fully disciplinary in our own right, composition runs the risk of housing its own isolated "body of knowledge" a risk that might limit its interaction with other disciplines. In other words, as a discipline, rhetoric and composition is in the awkward position of having a built-in "de-theorizer" that insists on practice, while at the same time, our desire to exist beyond the service role insists that we theorize in order to have our own "body of knowledge."

Undeniably, there is a need for further postmodern, particularly poststructuralist, theorizing that promotes pedagogy; these practice-driven theories have pushed composition studies closer to understanding itself as a field and have created a multiplicity of productive discussions about pedagogy that allow us to push at the borders of our service position. In the end, we must redefine the role of rhetoric and composition in the university, and postmodern composition theory is perhaps one catalyst to doing so. But at the same time, we cannot forget that while our tendency is to *apply* postmodern theory, many such theories were never intended to lead to any sort of application. The need for continued theorizing still exists.

TOWARD POSTSTRUCTURALIST, POSTMODERNIST THOUGHT

Theories constructed to challenge the more traditional structuralist paradigm now supersede other schools of thought in both literary studies and rhetoric and composition. Poststructuralism argues that language operates in arbitrary, noncodifiable ways. In other words, as Jonathan Culler explains, while "structuralists take linguistics as a model and attempt to develop grammars . . . that would account for the form and meaning of literary works," poststructuralists "investigate the way in which this project is subverted by the workings of the texts themselves" (22). Much of poststructuralist theory grows from the work of Ferdinand de Saussure, who, as Jane Tompkins writes, "is where post-structuralism starts" (734). Saussure grounds his work in the arbitrary nature of the sign. For Saussure, a sign is a concept—the "signified"—that is combined with a specific sound—what Saussure calls the "signifier." He posits that the relationship between the signified and the signifier is arbitrary; that is, there is no natural connection between the concept and the "sound image." The only correlation between the signifier and the signified is a relationship defined by convention. This arbitrary nature of language is a basic tenet of poststructuralist thought.

Drawing on Saussure's theory, Derrida radicalizes the arbitrary nature of language as he brings it to textual studies. Derrida "poststructuralizes" Saussure's work by pointing out that Saussure maintains a distinction between signifier and signified; that is, he gives the signified some kind of preexisting ontological status. For Derrida, however, once the signifier is peeled away, the signified does not remain in its place; rather, another layer of signifier assumes the position as will yet another signifier remain when the new signifier is removed. In other words, Derrida argues that signifiers can only represent a continuous string of more signifiers; never do we reach a true signified. Derrida argues that "there is no final resting place, no ground or reference that anchors the linguistic system in the self-presence of Being, truth, or meaning" (Harned 11). Sharon Crowley explains Derrida's position as a fairly esoteric strategy of reading developed . . . so that he could undertake a wide-ranging critique of Western philosophy. Derrida thinks that traditional philosophy binds and distorts thinking about the relations between self-consciousness, thought, and language. Traditional thought about these matters promotes a number of powerful and yet unspoken assumptions that have blinded Westerners to the deceptive nature of speech and writing and their role in human activities. The project called "deconstruction" attempts to expose these assumptions for what they are. (xvi)

Derrida's work identifies a tradition in Western thought that devalues writing, privileges spoken language, and recognizes the self as the center of human thought; Derrida calls this "the metaphysics of presence." According to Derrida, the metaphysics of presence posits that "as minds represent or signify the substances of nature, so does language represent or signify the 'stuff' of minds, and through this, nature" (Crowley 3).

For Derrida, in contrast to traditional ways of thinking, consciousness does not create, precede, or define language; rather, consciousness is constituted through language. In other words, traditional configurations of the mind/language relationship place language in a secondary position behind the mind as a tool that could only imitate the mind. Derrida subverts this hierarchy and claims, as Crowley explains, that "ability to signify—the ability which allowed the privileging of mind in the first place—was precisely the province or function of language" (5). It is through language, according to Derrida, that we come to know the mind. For Derrida, then, metaphysics becomes a myth, a construct of language.

Derrida recognizes the centrality of the metaphysical impulse to Western thought. Through deconstruction, as Crowley writes, "Derrida's project, here as elsewhere, is to de-sediment the metaphysical notions that inhere in and surround the important texts of western culture, to tease out and expose the strands of metaphysical web from which most of the western thought is suspended. In other words, he de-constructs the fiction that is metaphysics" (6). Derrida directs this project toward textual interpretation. He argues that a deconstructive reading does not necessarily search for a grand system of meaning that "makes sense" of a text. Nor does deconstruction search for a meaning in a text that existed for the author as the text was created. Rather, Derrida argues, "the reading must always aim at a certain relationship, unperceived by the writer, between what he commands and what he does not command of the patterns of language that he uses" (qtd. in Crowley 7). Deconstruction, then, according to Harned, "protests against logocentrism by breaking the interpretive constraints that hierarchies create" (13). More simply put, for Derrida, reading, writing, and all aspects of text production and interpretation become an issue of continued intertextuality and contextual engagement. Nowhere, according to deconstruction, can a text *have* meaning. Deconstruction, according to Barbara Johnson, is "the careful teasing out of warring forces of signification within the text"; deconstruction, then, is a kind of reading that both resists definitive meanings and also seeks out gaps or impasses in thought and language (5). Obviously, such notions have major implications for teachers and scholars of writing.

FOUCAULT'S ARCHAEOLOGY

Perhaps more relevant to composition than Derrida, who finds interpretive constraints on texts, Foucault offers post-structuralist theory that argues against similar constraints by "demonstrating their historical ubiquity" (Harned 13). For Foucault, interpretation is an issue of historical reserve. He is known particularly for his discussions of institution, power, and discourse, and compositionists who turn to postmodernist thought have become more and more interested in the intersections of power, knowledge, and discourse. With these concerns in mind, those scholars who draw on Foucault's work, often cite "The Discourse on Language" and "What Is an Author?" because of their obvious connection to composition. Less frequently, yet still consistently, *The History of Sexuality, Madness and Civilization: A History of Insanity in the Age of Reason, The Order of Things: An Archaeology of the Human Sciences*, and *Discipline and Punish: The Birth of the Prison* come to composition through discussions of ideology, institutions, knowledge making, and other issues that inform postmodernist thought. Although *The Archaeology of Knowledge* is not cited as frequently by compositionists as some of Foucault's other works, it nonetheless holds some important lessons for compositionists regarding discourse, categorization, and knowledge making.

Arguing that history, in our traditional understanding of it, takes the "monuments" of the past and transforms them into "documents," Foucault offers his *archaeology* as an attempt to trace things left by the past without a context. The consequence, Foucault argues, of regarding history as a chronological series of events is that history becomes limited to boundaries that do not take into account the relation or the contrast between events. Traditionally, history has been regarded as continuous, and, as such, history—the understanding of history—eliminates the roles of "decisions, accidents, initiatives, and discoveries" (8). In treating history this way, we lose sight of what Foucault calls the "total history"—a holistic way of looking at history—and instead focus on a "general history." Consequently, a methodological problem arises: how do we confront the continuously growing mass of documents that helps us define history? For Foucault, our understanding of history must be problematized, and he claims as the goal of *archaeology* to "uncover the principles and consequences of an autochthonous transformation that is taking place in the field of historical knowledge" (15).

Foucault argues that before the theoretical aspects of history can be explored we must first shake free of other notions that have dominated traditional historical thought: tradition, influence, development, evolution, spirit, categories, and unities. He contends that we must disconnect chronologies that lead us to finding starting points in history, and we must renounce themes that ensure the "infinite continuity of discourse" (25). All forms of continuity must not be discounted; rather, they must be placed in suspension while we disrupt the notions they have created. This process, Foucault claims, will free fields such as history from the confines of continuity. By freeing the "facts" of history from those groupings that purport to be natural unities, Foucault suggests that we can now describe particular discourses by means of controlled decisions.

For Foucault, statements are the basic element of discourse that can reflect categorizable ideas. That is, statements that are categorized in a specific group all share a similar thematic meaning. In order to describe how statements are related, Foucault addresses the relation between statements that have been confined to provisional groupings. He notes that statements that are determined to be political, economical, biological, psychopathological, and so on are forced into categories. This, he hypothesizes, occurs because statements, although different from one another in form and dispersed in time, form a group if they seem to refer to a single object or similar theme. He furthers this hypothesis by adding that similar form and type of "connexion" also create a need for grouping, as does determining a system for permanent and coherent concepts involved in the statements. However, he then posits that we should not seek out these themes but should create a field of strategic possibilities for relations between statements. By noting groupings called "medicine," "economics," and "grammar," Foucault attempts to show a need to find a reason for their unity.

In order to determine which "rules of formation" can be followed to allow for a field of relations, Foucault claims that we must first "map the *surfaces* of [objects'] *emergence*" (41). In addition, we must "describe the authorities of delimitation," and "we must analyze the *grids of specification*"—the systems by which objects are "divided, contrasted, related, regrouped, classified, and derived from one another" (41–42). In other words, Foucault attempts to determine on what groupings can be based. He recognizes that within a discourse of a group many similar phrases emerge, and he then attempts to identify what ties them together. He says that we first need to determine who is speaking: "Who, among the totality of speaking individuals, is accorded the right to use this sort of language (*langage*)? Who is qualified to do so?" (50). He adds that we must also describe the institutional *sites* from which the discourse comes and define the position the subject occupies in relation to the various groups.

Foucault continues his exploration of concepts by asking, "Could a law not be found that would account for the successive or simultaneous emergence of disparate concepts?" (56). He carefully notes that it would be difficult to trace the development of concepts; rather, we would have to organize the statements in which they are expressed. He points out that in doing so we must account for linear succession in which concepts appear, the configuration of how the statements are formulated, and the *procedure of intervention*, or the way in which concepts were transcribed. Foucault admits that in order to analyze such elements, he must rely on rules of formal construction and other rhetorical practices, but it is necessary to do so in order to determine grouping relationships. Giving the name *strategies* to recurring themes and theories in concepts, Foucault attempts to discover how strategies are distributed in history. He does not attempt to analyze specific themes or strategies—a job he says will require further study—but he instead argues that there is a need first to determine the possible *points of diffraction* of this discourse. He argues that not all groupings can be accounted for, so one must also describe all of the authorities that guide decisions into which fields one places a strategy. Furthermore, he notes that the distribution of strategies is also determined by the function the discourse plays.

Although he explains how he uses the term *statements* (he includes *objects*, *concepts*, and *strategies* as well), he recognizes a

need to define the word more thoroughly. He writes that at first observation a statement appears to be an "ultimate, undecomposable
element that can be isolated and introduced into a set of relations
with other similar elements" (80). However, he explains that such a
definition creates problems. If the statement is the elementary unit of
discourse, "what does it consist of?" (80). What is the difference
between a statement and a sentence? Do statements exist in any act of
formulation? Is more than a single statement necessary to formulate a
speech act? Since, Foucault argues, there are no structural criteria of
unity for the statement, it is useless to look for statements among
unitary groups of signs. Instead, the traditional *signifier* and *signified*
do not always exist when exploring statements, especially when the
statement is reduced to a single proper noun, such as "Peter!" Nouns,
Foucault claims, can occupy several positions in language at the
same time and therefore may constitute different meanings to different signifiees. He goes on to explain that a "statement also differs
from any series of linguistic elements by virtue of the fact that it possesses a particular relation with a subject" (92). Foucault also
attributes to the enunciative function that it "can operate without
the existence of an associated domain" (96). In other words, a statement does not need a sentence or proposition in order to exist.

Foucault asks of statements, "What do I now understand by the
task . . . of describing statements? How can this theory of the statement be adjusted to the analysis of discursive formations?" (106).
First, Foucault claims, the language needed to engage in statement
analysis must be defined; he pays careful attention to *linguistic performance* and *discourse* in relation to statements. Accordingly, a
statement is further explained to be an element that is not a unit that
can be added to the unities described by grammar or logic; instead,
characteristics of conditions which contribute to the configuration
must also be explored. Foucault continues his theory by applying
the statement to the analysis of discursive formations:

1. It can be said that the mapping of discursive formations,
   independently, of other principles of possible unification,
   reveals the specific level of the statement; but it can also
   be said that the description of statements and of the way in
   which the enunciative level is organized leads to the indi-
   vidualization of the discursive formation. . . .

2. A statement belongs to a discursive formation as a sentence belongs to a text, and a proposition to a deductive
   whole. . . .

3. So we can now give a full meaning to the definition of "discourse." . . . We shall call discourse a group of statements in so far as they belong to the same discursive formation. . . .

4. Lastly, we can define what we have called "discursive practice" . . . it is a body of anonymous, historical rules, always determined in the time and space that have defined a given period, and for a given social, economic, geographical, or linguistic area, the conditions of operation of the enunciative function. (116–17)

Foucault shows that the realm of discourse is virtually infinite and claims that it includes an element of rarity. He argues that while *everything* is never said, what *is* said establishes a law of rarity. He claims that in studying what is said in relation to what is not said we do not attempt to give voice to the surrounding silence but to account for the exclusions of what is said. He cautions that through "exclusions" we should not create a repression or suggest that what *is* said conceals a hidden agenda in what *is not* said. "This rarity of statements," he writes, "the incomplete, fragmented form of the enunciative field, the fact that few things, in all, can be said, explain that statements are not, like the air we breathe, an infinite transparency" (119–20).

Traditionally, Foucault argues, the history of discourse has dealt with two central values: traditional and original (old and new). Hence, he suggests that we can distinguish between two categories of formulation: those that are valued highly and considered rare and those that are considered ordinary and common. Identity of a statement, what is considered the origin of that statement, is generally not an important factor. Because Foucault's archaeological analysis looks at individual discursive formations in relation to other discursive formations, a comparison is forced. Yet, at the same time in archaeological analysis, comparison is limited and regional, and it does not create a rationality but a tangle that cannot be limited. In other words, archaeology attempts to uncover five primary tasks:

a. To show how quite different discursive elements may be formed on the basis of similar rules; to show, between different formations, the *archaeological isomorphisms.*

b. To show to what extent these rules do or do not apply in the same way, are or are not linked in the same order, are

or are not arranged in accordance with the same model in different types of discourse; to define the *archaeological model* of each formation.
c. To show how entirely different concepts occupy a similar position in the ramification of their system of posivity.
d. To show, on the other hand, how a single notion may cover two archaeologically distinct elements; to indicate the *archaeological shifts*.
e. Lastly, to show how, from one posivity to another, relations of subordination or complimentarily may be established; to establish the *archaeological correlations*. (160–61)

Archaeology, then, reveals relations between discursive formations and nondiscursive domains such as institutions and political events.

Yet, Foucault's potential contribution to composition theory is not limited to his analysis to archaeology. His discussions on discourse, power, institutions, and the role of the author seem to lead to natural implications for compositionists. In "What Is an Author?" he further argues for the historical relevance of discursive formations. And in doing so, he locates the importance of written discourse in historical context. He writes, "Even now, when we study the history of a concept, a literary genre, or a branch of philosophy, these concerns assume a relatively weak and secondary position in relation to the solid and fundamental role of an author and his works" (115). The poststructural notion of discontinuative history and its impact on and through language contribute to the disruption of traditional logocentric views of knowledge and self. As I will discuss in a moment, because these poststructuralist theories seem to lend themselves to composition, several compositionists, including Herzberg and Spellmeyer, have tried to make direct links between Foucault's theories and practical composition applications, just as other scholars have attempted to bring other poststructuralist theories to the composition classroom.

CONTENDING WITH POSTSTRUCTURALISM IN COMPOSITION

The works of Foucault, Derrida, and other poststructuralist theorists raise serious questions concerning discourse, questions which have great ramifications for composition and for ways in which we view the field. Compositionists have found various ways both to embrace and reject postmodernism. For instance, James Berlin sees postsmodernist pedagogies as leading to the liberation of students' consciousnesses; Berlin argues that when these pedagogies are employed in composition classrooms, students learn to examine daily experience in order to recognize their false consciousness (491–92). Like Berlin, Bizzell also seeks to employ poststructuralist ideas in the composition classroom to raise the critical consciousness of her students. For Bizzell, composition classrooms need to move away from cognitivism and current-traditional paradigms and to recognize that "to point out that discourse conventions exist would be to politicize the classroom" ("Cognition" 99). In fact, Bizzell posits that practices in the composition classroom should be overtly political in order to teach students to become critically conscious of the cultural hegemony that helps define discourse.[2] Likewise, scholars such as Covino, Crowley, Louise Whetherbee Phelps, Schilb, and Sosnoski have all found close ties between poststructuralist theory and composition studies. We clearly see the influence postmodernism has on composition through important texts such as G. Douglas Atkins and Michael L. Johnson's *Writing and Reading Differently: Deconstruction and the Teaching of Composition and Literature* and Jasper Neel's *Plato, Derrida, and Writing*. Works such as Gregory Ulmer's *Applied Grammatology: Post(e)-Pedagogy from Jacques Derrida to Joseph Beuys* have been critiqued and discussed at length for their application of postmodernist theory to pedagogy. On the other hand, compositionists such as Jim Corder, W. Ross Winterowd, Ann Berthoff, and Hairston have found fault with composition's postmodern turn. Like any new intellectual development in the field, postmodernism has become a site of debate in composition.

As scholars attempt to work out ways in which poststructuralist theory is or is not beneficial to composition, several interesting considerations have been brought to the fore. For instance, Schilb posits that one way to evaluate the merit of poststructuralism is "to compare the 'traditions of inquiry'" between it and composition ("Tale" 423). He asks, "What should be the relation between the new discipline of composition and the poststructuralist thinking that has developed alongside it in the past twenty years?" ("Tale" 436). In answering his own question, Schilb argues that the two can operate as critique of each other. He writes, "Composition can prod advocates of poststructuralism to consider purpose, context, and material result in the analysis of human utterance, while poststructuralists can remind compositionists that vulnerable presuppositions underlie even the most avowedly pragmatic stance" ("Tale" 436–37). And yet, while

Schilb sees direct links between poststructuralism and composition, the connections he attempts to achieve in "Composition and Post-structuralism: A Tale of Two Conferences" are not as clear-cut as he would propose.

In *Contending with Words: Composition and Rhetoric in a Postmodern Age*, a collection of essays, Schilb and Harkin present works that are strongly influenced by postmodernist thought and that more thoroughly address the problems of composition's encounter with postmodernism and poststructuralism. In the introduction, Harkin and Schilb write that the essays in this collection "do not fall easily into categories of postmodernist thought. Nor can they easily be understood in terms of a theory-practice opposition. None is 'theory-pure.' Each addresses pedagogical questions" (6). This assessment of the essays addresses a prominent concern about the ways in which postmodernist discourse is making its way into composition. As I discuss in Chapter One, theoretical knowledge has traditionally been a privileged knowledge. Yet, the editors of this collection seem to argue that postmodern theory and composition pedagogy operate in some sort of dialectical relationship; the essays approach both theoretical and practical issues. *Contending with Words*, then, becomes an attempt to find ways in which postmodern theory engages composition's pedagogical concerns. If this well-received collection is representative of a growing concern in composition, then it would appear that many compositionists are quite receptive to the idea of postmodern theory as catalyst for new composition pedagogies. These theories, shunned as "off-the-wall" by many of our more traditional scholars, are being employed in composition in some very productive ways.

Several essays in *Contending with Words*—such as Harkin's, Schilb's, and Victor Vitanza's—address the theory/practice debate from a postmodern perspective. Harkin, for instance, writes that "In the American Academy, research is understood to produce knowledge on a more or less scientistic model, while service courses provide practical instruction in the application of that knowledge" (124–25). In other words, Harkin recognizes the traditional split between theoretical research and practical application. She goes on to write, "The recent attention to teaching, by contrast, seeks to demonstrate that teaching itself makes knowledge in ways that are different from, but not less valuable than, the methods of science" (125). Harkin seems to be arguing here for the same sort of dialectical interaction that she and Schilb call for in the introduction in that she argues for a balance in the status we accord different forms of knowledge. For Harkin, both practical and theoretical knowledge serve equal purpose in composition studies.

At the same time, as Sosnoski explains, Harkin attempts—along with other contributors to *Contending with Words*—to redefine rhetoric in postmodern terms. For Harkin, restructuring our views of rhetoric comes through our professional lore. She draws on Stephen North's idea of *lore*, practical knowledge that is "nondisciplinary: it is actually defined by its inattention to disciplinary procedures. Lore cannot provide abstract accounts of the writing act; it tells us what practitioners do" (125). According to Harkin, lore records what occurs in practical scenarios and these accounts are more applicable than published theoretical endeavors. Lore for Harkin resists the traditional discipline of composition. Harkin exemplifies this resistance in her analysis of John Rouse's account of Mina Shaughnessy's work. As Sosnoski explains, Harkin shows how "Rouse imposes disciplinary criteria on Shaughnessy's description of her lore" (204). For Harkin, theory is tailored to find classroom use; lore, then, comprises the accounts of theories that work. As Sosnoski notes, however, lore is not formed pragmatically:

> It is contradictory. It disobeys the law of noncontradiction. It is eclectic. It takes feelings and emotions into account. It is subjective and nonreplicable. It is not binary. It counts as knowing only in a postdisciplinary context. Whether it counts is a political issue with many consequences. (204)

Harkin's view of lore places composition in a postmodern light. Lore questions knowledge and certainly disrupts structural perceptions about composition by questioning the role theory plays in the development of specific practices. Or as Sosnoski writes, "A postmodern view of discourse redefines the subject matter of any course in rhetoric. It also invites us to abandon the notion that rhetoric is merely a servant" (203). This is a political conception of how compositionists produce knowledge.

Vitanza also argues for a perception of theory and practice in composition that does not allow either form of knowledge to stagnate. In order to promote organic theory and practice, Vitanza draws on Jean-François Lyotard's debate with Jürgen Habermas and the recent works of Gilles Deleuze and Félix Guattari to construct his three countertheses of "perverse comedy." For Vitanza, perverse comedy is not a "mere attack on the status quo but a meditative questioning of it through an act of ironic 'critical in(ter)vention'" (139). He writes of perverse comedy:

It is both critical and an in(ter)vention here in that uncanny criticisms will be deployed heuristically with the sole purpose of establishing the (postmodern) conditions for the possibilities of discourse in and about writing theory and pedagogy that, heretofore, the field of composition has had to disallow. Perverse comedy is an attempt at a discourse, therefore, that requires itself to bear witness to what has been disallowed by searching for comedic counteridioms that will allow, that will enable. At times, however, this discourse is not easy to follow, for it attempts a discourse that does not follow. (139–40)

Vitanza offers three countertheses: the first "(de)centers on the age-old issue of whether knowledge can be legitimized or grounded either on some universal, ontogenetic theory (that is, on some universal law or *physis*) or rhetorically on consensus theory (that is, on homology, or local *nomoi*)" (145). This first thesis is counter to traditional structuralism and foundationalism. In his critique of absolute epistemologies, Vitanza writes:

Either there can no longer be or that ethically, micropolitically, there should not be any foundational principle or covering law or ontogenetic model for composition theory and pedagogy. It does not matter whether that principle is based on a conceptual theory or a tropology of composition (D'Angelo), on a cognitive/computer model (Flower and Hayes), on a universal pragmatics (speech acts) of rational communication (Habermas; Kinneavy, *Theory*), or on social consensus, social construction of reality, or interpretive communities (Bizzell; Bartholomae). (148)

Vitanza's second thesis "centers on the Nietzchean-Freudian question Who speaks when something is spoken? (It is a question of author[ship])" (152). Vitanza explains that in the humanist tradition, "human beings speak" (152). Yet, as he says, drawing on Lyotard, there is a question as to how language operates for "addressor or addressee" (152). In other words, Vitanza's second thesis questions, by way of Lyotard, the role of language.

According to Vitanza, "The third counterthesis is more of an indirect meditation on the consequences of the Habermas-Lyotard debate (which we are steadily leaving behind, so as to drift on).

Specifically, it states (from a postmodern, 'third sophistic' perspective) that theory as the game of knowledge cannot help as a resource, because theory of this sort resists finally being theorized, totalized" (159). Vitanza, then, questions totalizing narratives and, in turn, assumes the postmodern critique of theory: that it cannot, in composition, serve as foundational knowledge for constructing pedagogies. What makes this position interesting is that Vitanza—like many who draw on postmodern theory to engage composition—employs postmodernist ideas in order to critique postmodernism. Postmodern theory, particularly poststructuralism, lends itself to self-reflexive critique, and, for compositionists, this seems to be an important characteristic of these theories.

Drawing more directly on postmodernist thought, Schilb in his essay "Cultural Studies, Postmodernism, and Composition," looks closely at the ways in which composition imports postmodernist ideas. This essay is particularly telling of the field's general perception of postmodern theory and its value in composition. In this essay, Schilb emphasizes the ways in which the terms *postmodernism* and *cultural studies* operate in composition. He writes that four developments have helped the field of literary studies move toward poststructuralist thought. First, he argues, poststructuralist criticism has been used enough by literary scholars over time that scholars in other fields have begun to recognize how it can "illuminate other discourses besides literature if pushed in their direction and infected with greater social consciousness" (174). Second, traditional boundaries and categories begin to break down as literary theorists borrow from various disciplines in order to develop poststructuralist thought. Third, the vast numbers of students representing multiple cultures and backgrounds have forced literature teachers to reevaluate the value and relevance of "traditional texts and pedagogies" (174). Finally, Schilb contends that there is an increase in connection between literacy scholarship and the thinking of marginalized groups: feminists, minorities, the economically disadvantaged, homosexuals, and so on. As these developments in postmodernist thinking evolve, postmodern theorists, Schilb notes, "must keep in mind that the term can designate a critique of traditional epistemology, a set of artistic practices, and an ensemble of larger social conditions" (174). In other words, postmodernist thinking lends itself to critique of traditional ways of making knowledge. So, as Schilb argues in "Composition and Poststructuralism: A Tale of Two Conferences," poststructuralist thought serves as a self-reflexive critique of traditional thought; this is the same argument by which Derrida developed deconstruction as a critique of traditional Western epistemologies. What bearing, then, does this work have specifically on composition as a young field that participates in knowledge making?

For Schilb, composition becomes a site where postmodernism (arm in arm with cultural studies) can more readily, and more beneficially, flourish. However, he cautions:

> Several of us in the emerging field of composition have grown just as interested as literature colleagues in cultural studies and postmodernism and how they may relate. Indeed, I think our field can even more powerfully illuminate these two terms and examine the wisdom of linking them. Yet we should not automatically ingest a particular version of either; instead, through our scholarship and pedagogy we should ponder issues of the sort I mention here. A composition program would therefore examine various theories of cultural studies and postmodernism as well as how they diverge or mesh. ("Postmodern" 175)

What is striking about this passage is that, while citing composition as a field ripe for pursuing postmodernism, Schilb again does so in a manner that suggests that postmodern theory must operate in a dialectical relationship with postmodern pedagogy. He specifically posits that postmodernist thinking must be pursued through scholarship (theory) *and* pedagogy (practice). He writes, "Composition is well suited for this inquiry. Because the field currently comprises diverse topics and methods and has ties to numerous disciplines, it can analyze broad social questions better than literary studies can" ("Postmodern" 176). Hence, Schilb sees postmodern theory as a useful tool in composition studies, though he believes that this "does not mean that composition ought to claim final authority" over postmodernism ("Postmodern" 176).

Schilb identifies several reasons *why* composition seems to be an appropriate field for the development of postmodern theory. Like Harkin and Vitanza, Schilb identifies a positive relationship between postmodern theoretical developments and composition both as practice and as scholarship:

> Composition can embody the preoccupation with discourse associated with cultural studies and postmodernism. Both

have evoked various cultural phenomena as texts; hence, a field identified with broad textual inquiry seems quite relevant to them. Composition's rhetorical bent has, in fact, grown more pertinent as certain theorists of these terms have questioned theory's generalizing bent and stressed that discourse operates in particular conjunctures. ("Postmodern" 176)

Yet for Schilb, composition's interaction with postmodernism exists not as a current engagement but as potential, a potential "we are far from recognizing, because of institutional and ideological factors embedded in composition's past" ("Postmodern" 177). He recognizes that traditionally composition has been viewed as a service to the university, a field dedicated and "invented purely to train students in the mechanics of language, to help them face the newly specialized demands of higher education and the emerging circumstances of corporate life" ("Postmodern" 177–78). At the same time, however, Schilb's recognition of the role postmodernism could play in composition scholarship as well as pedagogy suggests that he sees beyond this limited view of the discipline; it suggests that he recognizes the importance of theoretical development in rhetoric and composition. He sees beyond the "ethos that envelops composition to this day: a belief that it exists only to serve the 'real' disciplines, which are best served when composition focuses on students' 'basic skills'" ("Postmodern" 178). Schilb, in fact, argues that composition can promote postmodern theories in ways that are especially beneficial to postmodernism, more critical of Western epistemologies while simultaneously promoting greater social awareness of composition as a discipline.

It is precisely this introduction of postmodern theory into composition that will promote theoretical developments of these schools of thought while at the same time extending our understanding of composition. As I mentioned in Chapter One, if we are to view rhetoric and composition solely as a service field dedicated to teaching skills to students for the benefit of the rest of the university, then, certainly, postmodern and poststructuralist theory might not serve any *real* role in our discipline—except, perhaps in limited ways. However, for those of us who recognize rhetoric and composition as a field ripe with possibility for exploring the myriad functions of discourse, then engaging composition with postmodern theory serves to benefit composition, composition instruction, and, in turn, the evolution of postmodern and poststructuralist theories.

APPLYING FOUCAULT

While scholars such as Bizzell, Harkin, Schilb, and Vitanza discuss theoretical issues concerning the use of postmodern theory in composition, several scholars have attempted to apply such theory in practical ways or have at least examined its potential application. Some of these discussions involve Foucault's work. Because Foucault's theories are so diverse and exist as theories that do not seem to lean toward application, many have claimed that one cannot "do" Foucault, or, as my epigraph from *The Times* suggests, one cannot be a Foucaultian. For example, in their introductory discussion of Foucault as a poststructural theorist, Robert Con Davis and Ronald Schleifer remark that Foucault's work does not lend itself to situational application (263). For the most part, Foucault's work teaches us much about the operations of discourse but does not necessarily lend itself to direct practical application. Even in composition, Foucault has earned a place as one of our most cited scholars, yet little has been offered in ways of translating his theories into pedagogies. As Herzberg points out, "Composition scholars have cited Foucault dutifully as a powerful influence on modern epistemological skepticism, but he seems to have had little place in the classroom" (80). While scholars such as Burton Hatlen recognize the importance of Foucault's work in our understanding of the field as a whole (see "Michel Foucault and the Discourse[s] of English"), three notable attempts to enhance pedagogies with Foucault's work come from Herzberg, Spellmeyer, and Carol Snyder. Current scholarship, such as Gail Stygall's 1994 *CCC* article "Resisting Privilege: Basic Writing and Foucault's Author Function" continues to find ways to bring Foucault's theories to composition pedagogies.

In "Michel Foucault's Rhetorical Theory," Herzberg posits that Foucault's discussions of history, discourse, knowledge, disciplines, institutions, and other social constructs address "some of the deepest concerns of modern rhetoric and composition theory" (69). Herzberg points out that in Foucault's theory of discourse there is a close relation between discourse and knowledge, and he shows how Foucault describes

the functions of disciplines, institutions, and other discourse communities in producing discourse, knowledge, and power; he examines the ways that particular statements come to have truth-value, the material constraints on the production

of discourse about objects of knowledge, the effects of discursive practices on social action, and the uses of discourse
to exercise power. (69)

Herzberg also addresses ways in which Foucault "locates the central
dilemma of discourse at a point in history that reveals the connection
between what he calls 'discourse' and what we may wish to call
'rhetoric'" (69).

In his reading of Foucault, Herzberg defines "true discourse" as
that which

embodies and creates truth because the truth it speaks is
social, a truth of persuasion, decision, political power, justice, and cultural cohesion. . . . Discourse always conveys
something other than itself . . . it is not the act of discourse
but the signified object of discourse that determines
whether the discourse is true. What Foucault calls "the will
to truth." (70)

Drawing on Foucault's "Order of Discourse" (or "The Discourse on
Language"), Herzberg discusses the truth-making aspects of discourse
and how "its power was hidden by a will to truth whose object was
conceived to be absolute and immutable, not social, not contingent,
not conventional, not affected by language" (71).

In *The Order of Things*, Foucault explores the ways discourse
was effaced and made to appear transparent. By exploring Foucault's
treatment in *The Archaeology of Knowledge* of the role of the speaker,
the formation of concepts, and the formation of strategies, Herzberg
demonstrates ways in which Foucault rejects the "traditional
assumption that objects account for the unity of a discourse" (74).
Foucault is more concerned with answering questions regarding who
speaks in discourse. Herzberg similarly asks, "What institutional
role, legal status, social privilege, educational certification, and so on
determines who may claim the right to speak authoritatively?" (74).
But what impact do Foucault's questions (and answers) have on composition pedagogy? While Herzberg does not offer a step-by-step
heuristic for teaching composition based on Foucault, he does offer
some important ties between Foucault's teachings and composition
pedagogy.

Herzberg writes, "In the context of composition in particular,
one implication of accepting Foucault's ideas is that we must reevaluate the several types of local contexts for rhetorical analysis—author,

audience, oeuvre, even general historical knowledges" (79). In other words, bringing Foucault to the classroom encourages us to reevaluate ways in which we produce and exchange knowledge, an action Foucault would deem as social. Foucault recognizes discourse production to be a social action, yet according to Herzberg, Foucault's work "does not automatically endorse socially oriented pedagogies" (79). Rather, Herzberg, by way of Foucault, argues that when students collaborate they do so more with the social institutions to which they are confined—the university, for example—than they actually do with each other. More simply put, Herzberg's critique questions collaborative pedagogical methods—and social-constructionist pedagogies in general—and their attempt to secure a "closer approximation to the way that knowledge is *really* formed" (79). For Herzberg, Foucault's theories are extremely useful to compositionists because they raise "explicit questions about the effects of relying on experience, concepts, and so on as premises about the source of knowledge" (79).

As Herzberg sees it, composition teachers must negotiate between a need for closure, a need for practical production of writing, and an openness of continued inquiry. Within this contradiction, Herzberg posits that compositionists, then, may have dual projects: "One is to analyze more closely the role of our institutions and disciplines in producing discourse, knowledge, and power (a process many have advanced by heeding the extant analyses of critical educationists). The other is, of course, to find a place for a critical agenda in the classroom" (80). Here, Herzberg seems to be arguing for the usefulness of Foucault's work on two levels: practical and theoretical.

Herzberg is specific in his need to find ways in which Foucault can be applied to classroom practices. He, like so many others in composition, finds value in theory when it can be applied. However, at the same time, he recognizes the need to pursue Foucault's work from a theoretical stance as well. Again, Herzberg sees a need for a dialectical link between theory and practice in composition. He writes, "If, with Foucault, we reject the theory that language is the servant of knowledge in favor of the theory that discourse constitutes knowledge and its powers, we may be able to reconstitute our composition courses under the rubric of a new rhetoric" (81). Herzberg's point is clear: an understanding of theory can lead to a better conception of pedagogy.

Similarly, Spellmeyer, in "Foucault and the Freshman Writer: Considering the Self in Discourse," finds several links between Foucault's theory and practical strategies for first-year composition instructors. Like Herzberg, Spellmeyer draws on Foucault's consideration of what constitutes knowledge. Spellmeyer turns to Foucault's "game of truth" and the problem of the speaking "I." For Spellmeyer, "Discourse does not assign to the subject a definitive role, like an actor's part on the stage or the moves available to a pawn on the chessboard" (716). Hence, Spellmeyer believes that we "cannot really teach writing at all, cannot show students how to construct themselves in language" (716).

Drawing from "The Discourse on Language," Spellmeyer argues that Foucault's aim "is not, as some readers have argued, to reveal the hidden structures determining the production of knowledge, but to expose a fundamental contradiction between the nature of knowledge and the notion of 'lawful' unchanging structures" (717). Spellmeyer notes, "By showing us how games of truth are really played—by showing us the tensions underlying the reasoned calm, the conflict behind the apparent detachment—Foucault invites us to contest our disadvantages or exclusion, our subjugation within knowledge" (717). Spellmeyer takes this to mean that language uses students just as they believe they can animate their intentions through language. He recognizes the constraints discourse imposes on the "speaking subject" and posits that "the world of academic discourse is especially precarious because its posture of methodical objectivity demands the concealment of those transgressions which are as essential to learning as they are to the formation of new knowledge. Nowhere is it more true than in the university that 'we are not,' in Foucault's words, 'free to say just anything' ('Discourse' 216)" (718). He criticizes ways in which compositionists have used Foucault to defend "the normative stability of discourse, at the expense of both the writer's situation and the eventfulness of language itself. They perceive Foucault's 'who is speaking?' simply as a question about the institutional orthodoxy of an utterance, its approval by a body of recognized practitioners" (720).

Bringing his use of Foucault to the classroom, Spellmeyer writes:

> To find a voice inside a community of speakers we must concurrently pursue the thought from the outside. While there is, of course, no transcendental subjectivity, every event of language reconstitutes a speaking self as the "I," present implicitly or explicitly, which cannot "slip imperceptibly" into the flow of words that precedes it. Only this "I" this always "exterior" self with its ability to change can furnish the inconsistency discourse requires.

> Inconsistency and transgression may have a place in composition theory, but they typically stand at the farthest remove from actual practice. (721).

He continues, "We postpone discourse in the name of discourse when we silence those exterior voices our students bring to class without knowing it, voices from the home and from the past, nearly forgotten, which our alien words might reanimate" (722). Using examples of his students' writing, he illustrates how student writers frequently display that the common notion that students must know what they believe before they can speak is untrue. He argues that Foucault demonstrates how the opposite is actually true: "We speak first, and then learn what we have said and whom we have become. By beginning and beginning again, attempting and being mistaken, the 'I' defines a space it can occupy, long before the writer makes any conscious determinations about truth and falsity, consistency or inconsistency, understanding or misunderstanding" (723). In other words, as Spellmeyer explains, "While writing can become a 'practice of freedom,' no writer is unconstrained by other voices, by discursive conventions, by institutional regulations" (724). For Spellmeyer, then, Foucault offers composition instructors insight into how language constructs self and thereby helps us see that we may limit expression of self by limiting student discourse. Like Herzberg's, Spellmeyer's pedagogy is not necessarily a heuristic for teaching models, though he does make some strong ties between Foucault's theories and classroom practices. Very few of the scholars who bring Foucault's work to the classroom do actually offer specific strategies for the classroom; however, Snyder, unlike Herzberg and Spellmeyer, does.

In her essay, "Analyzing Classifications: Foucault for Advanced Writing," Snyder offers an "approach to teaching classification based on the work of Michel Foucault . . . a set of principles for understanding classification . . . and a plan of inquiry students can use both to generate working theses about classification and to improve the classifications they themselves propose" (209–10). In her introductory statement, Snyder's agenda is apparent: to make use of Foucault's work to create a working strategy to help students understand classification. She is clearly attempting to translate theory into useable practice.

Snyder explains that "Foucault's histories abound in examples of the power of classifications to shape intellectual and social reality, examples that should prove provocative to students and teachers overly familiar with the biological model of classification on which so many writing texts rely" (210). Returning to Foucault's "author function" and other questions of authority and power, Snyder schematizes his work and designs a pedagogy based directly on his work. In her pedagogy, Snyder opens classroom discussion by defining *classification*, the ways in which strategies of classification permeate both discourse and institutions, and the ways that the act of classifying influences historical reality. As a general principle, Snyder tells her students, *"classifications both reflect and direct our thinking. The way we order represents the way we think"* (211). She goes on to write that pedagogically

> The best way to bring this principle home to students, I have found, is to present them with two subsidiary propositions and some examples. The first proposition is that *we classify only what we consider important: the rise of a taxonomy identifies a new topic of conceptual importance.* . . . For the second proposition, I use a statement from paleontologist Stephen Jay Gould from an article of his reviewing Foucault's work: *"Historical changes in classification are the fossilized indicators of conceptual revolution."* (211)

Snyder's second principle focuses on the power relations between classifications and their objects: *"classifications have the power to dispose their objects"* (212). In other words, according to Snyder, by classifying an object, we isolate that object. For instance, "discursive classifications isolate objects of knowledges; institutions, when they classify their human objects, regulate them as well, assigning them to partitioned locales like hospital wards, classrooms, and prison cells" (211).

Following this introduction to classification, Snyder has prepared a system of inquiry based on these principles and on Foucault's questions regarding discourse. Snyder first asks her students to *"identify the object of the classification"* (212). She asks her students to inquire as to "what is being classified? Does the classification affect human beings? How?" (212). Her intent here is to "remind students to consider the social implications of some ordering schemes" (212). Next she has students *"identify what the classification excludes"* (213). Questioning exclusion, Snyder believes, helps students "see that the criteria used to establish privileged categories are sometimes slanted" (213). Third, Snyder encourages students to *"identify the human subjects who devise or use the classification"* (213). By offering a series of questions that guide students in this part of the inquiry, Snyder hopes that "probing the authority of classifiers can help students uncover the not always obvious perspectives that classifiers bring to their tasks" (213). Next, Snyder asks students to "*locate the classification in time*," a task she sees as helping students ask "broader questions about the history of the classification" (214). Finally, Snyder has students "*locate the classification in space*" (214). In other words, Snyder wants students to consider where the classification was formulated and what social sites and institutions make use of that classification.

Tying her system of inquiry to writing tasks, Snyder argues:

> By preparing students to seek meanings, the plan of inquiry provides an essential stimulus to good writing. As they engage with these five groups of questions, students come to see that the classifications that order their disciplines are meaningful human inventions with significant effects, that they are, in fact, *open* to question and explanation, and thus that writing about them might lead to useful discoveries. (215)

She encourages her students to engage these questions in their writing, and she posits that by doing so students are more likely to classify in their own writing:

> This approach to teaching classification should help students find their way around the classified spaces of their disciplines and demystify for them one of the basic forms of academic discourse. At the same time, asking and answering the questions Foucault raises can lead students to understand that the construction of classifications, like the production of academic knowledge in general, is strongly affected by and strongly affects social conditions. (215–16)

Here, like others who bring postmodern and poststructuralist theories to composition, Snyder's ultimate goal lies in the recognition, awareness, and disruption of hegemonic discourse. Her concern, like Herzberg's and Spellmeyer's, goes beyond simple writing instruction to a form of critical consciousness that helps students become aware of ways in which social institutions affect language and vice versa.[3] In doing so, the pedagogies that Snyder, Herzberg, and Spellmeyer offer help students gain better control of their world through understanding how writing influences and reflects their world.

Foucault offers some powerful insights into the operation of discourse. When scholars such as Herzberg, Spellmeyer, and Snyder engage Foucault in ways that organically, dialectically bring his theories to composition, there is seemingly an acknowledgement that to some degree his theories *can* be translated into effective pedagogies. By recognizing this, scholars seem to be arguing that in order for Foucault to be of benefit to composition, we must somehow be able to find practical application in his theories. However, since scholars frequently cite Foucault in instances not pertaining directly to pedagogies, we also clearly see the theoretical value of his work. In composition we freely admit that Foucault has had great impact on how we view discourse, institutions, and so on. However, unlike most of the work in theory that we engage, Foucault's does not become easily entrapped in the traditional theory/practice debates. It is very difficult for us to derive pedagogies from his work; this is seen clearly in the fact that only a few scholars have attempted to do so. However, our frequent reference to his work suggests that we openly embrace his theory as important to our scholarship. Hence, Foucault becomes for composition an important figure in that his work is one of the few projects that compositionists willingly accept without insisting on a direct tie to pedagogy in all scenarios.

FINDING BALANCE BETWEEN THEORY AND PRAXIS IN COMPOSITION

While many compositionists have battled with the theoretical role postmodernism and poststructuralism (will) play in composition, several scholars such as Snyder have made direct attempts to create pedagogies from these theories. Such approaches to "doing theory" have the potential to be disastrous. However, in order to find ways in which poststructuralist or postmodern theory can be directly beneficial to compositionists, it is necessary to find ties between these new theories and our postmodern views of writing and the writing classroom.

In *Composition as a Human Science: Contributions to the Self-Understanding of a Discipline*, Phelps claims that "composition awakens in the initial moment of its disciplinary project to find itself already situated, prereflectively, within a specific cultural field of meaning—that of postmodernist thought, with its characteristic preoccupations and world vision" (3). Drawing on her own vision of how postmodernism and composition intersect, Phelps offers several practical applications that make use of postmodernist thought. For instance, she argues for an "integrative approach to the analysis of written language that would recognize the intersubjective source of meanings in text" (166). Here, she posits that texts elicit both receptive and interpretive responses. Phelps argues that in order for a text to accomplish both types of responses, there must be an inherent framework of linguistic and collective conventions in the text that reflect a shared social overlapping of knowledge. Yet, to achieve this overlap, certain skills must be contributed by both author and audience, though the focus of action must come from the reader. In her model of this "interpretive-constructive" view, Phelps offers six generalizations. First, "Readers bring to texts various kinds of knowledge, beliefs, and values on the one hand, and know-how—the skills of reading—on the other." Second, "Readers inhabit ongoing situations relevant to their readings, from which they approach texts with a purpose or set of purposes" (167). These first two characteristics of text interpretation draw directly on a postmodern, specifically deconstructive, theory of text interpretation. In doing so, Phelps suggests that these characteristics offer practioners direct insight into practical uses for postmodern theory.

The third and fourth characteristics listed in Phelps's model concentrate on the idea that we cannot assume that "readers aim for coherent experiences of all texts." The third characteristic argues that "Assuming the basic goal of comprehension, the reader's primary task is to make global sense of a text by constructing situational models of its content. Readers must grasp both the referential situation, the world a text describes or points to, and the rhetorical or communicative situation in which they are participating" (167). Fourth, Phelps posits that "Situational models are realized as global structures of meaning (macrostructures) that holistically define, interpret, and integrate local structures (microstructures) as their component meanings" (167).

Phelps argues that written discourse must be divided into "higher, more global levels of structure—the topics, themes, and ideas dominating paragraphs and longer stretches of text; and the lower or local levels—meanings derived from phrases and sentences" (167). However, Phelps does not take this so far as to argue that in every textual interpretive situation a reader will construct complete and accurate representations of meaning; this is dependent upon the individual and the individual situation. In other words, Phelps seems to be arguing for an interpretive relativism—the same sort of interpretive relativism that both Derrida and Foucault would acknowledge from different sources in poststructuralist thought. This position is also reflective of the anti-foundationalism that frightens so many from poststructuralism. Phelps' relative interpretation of textual encounter elicits from many a fear that texts no longer have *meanings*. Or as Blum comments, "the poststructural commitment to textuality . . . results in a strong tendency toward epistemological antifoundationalism, an intellectual skepticism characterized by thoroughgoing relativism" (93). Phelps instead insists that textual interpretation is dependent not only on the individual reader but also on the independent moment to which the reader comes to the text. She writes:

> Readers comprehend texts through progressive integration, projecting an anticipatory holistic structure that they continually reform, clarify, enrich, and fill in to whatever degree fits their goals and capabilities. At the same time they abstract and simplify this structure in retrospect, both as they read through the text and later in rereading and memory. (169)

She concludes:

> No matter how extensive their effort and constructive contribution, readers ascribe the integrated meanings derived in reading to the text that cues them, and beyond that to the writer who composed them, so long as they feel they can correlate such meanings globally with a writer's intention. (169)

Certainly, at the outset, this model seems to be simply a recap of reader-response mixed with Derridean deconstruction and with several other postmodern theories. However, in light of Phelps's overall goal—to explore how teaching interacts with inquiry and reflection—this model spells out some direct ties between postmodern theory and practice. For instance, this model suggests, as Phelps does earlier in her work, that "we have grounds for enlarging the teaching responsibilities of composition to encompass the origins of literacy in cultural experience and its continuing growth and application to practical contexts, such as work or public life, within the individual's personal history" (71).

While Phelps's overall goal is admirable, her conclusions regarding the interactive roles of postmodern theory and practice seem to be slightly skewed. Phelps recognizes that "theory and praxis mutually discipline each other" (238). Yet, she attributes an equality to them in an attempt at balance, a balance that perhaps could be as counterproductive as lack of interaction between theory and practice. She writes, "The broader goal of this analysis was to strike a new balance between theory and praxis, acknowledging the purposes and values of both theorists constructing a discipline and teachers enacting a practice" (238). She continues:

> I have tried to demonstrate how praxis disciplines Theory, because for a theorist that is a less obvious truth, and because I came to see that it was necessary to attack the naive logocentrism that gave Theory hegemony over praxis. Praxis disciplines Theory by demonstrating its limits, destroying its absolutist pretensions to be the sole foundation and ultimate reality on which practice depends. (239)

And, finally, Phelps asks, "If Theory cannot tell teachers what to do, what good is it to them?" (239). Phelps demands a direct link between theory and praxis. She too, despite her attempt at engaging theory/practice as a dialectical relationship, attributes a service quality to composition that requires theory to exist for the sake of practice. Her balance dissolves productive tension and debate and eliminates necessary theoretical endeavor that helps us understand language without necessarily influencing pedagogy.

POSTMODERNISM AND DIALOGIC PEDAGOGY

In *The Art of Wondering: A Revisionist Return to the History of Writing*, William Covino introduces a history of rhetoric based on postmodernist thought because, "How we read the history of rhetoric, and what we read, and the implications for teaching we derive, can change" (2). In doing so, Covino concludes his work with "some general propositions—'lessons of history'—for teachers" (3). For Covino, the lessons of history seem to hold great insight for pedagogies, and his pedagogical approach has come to be recognized as one of the major attempts at bringing postmodern theory to pedagogical applications.

Drawing on the works of Plato, Aristotle, Cicero, Montaigne, Vico, Hume, Blair, Byron, DeQuincy, and the more recent contributions of Derrida, Feyerabend, and Geertz, Covino remaps the tradition of rhetorical studies in a critique of traditional approaches to these thinkers. For instance, Covino claims that traditional understanding of Plato's and Aristotle's rhetorical theories "reified their works into lists of rules and principles that are respectively associated with 'Platonic' or 'Aristotelian' rhetoric" (33). He argues that, in fact, "Plato was not a Platonist and Aristotle not an Aristotelian" (33). Rather, as Ward points out, "Covino's rereading of Plato, Aristotle, and Cicero recovers the aspects of their works that value ambiguity, open-endedness, and multiple perspectives"—all cherished postmodern values (135–36). For Covino, postmodernism opens doors to multiple perspectives in the writing classroom. Envisioning a postmodern composition classroom and questioning the emphasis the discipline has placed on product, purpose, and closure, Covino calls for a "philosophy of composition that exploits writing as a mode of *avoiding* rather than *intending* closure, a philosophy of composition informed by the lessons of a revisionist history, a philosophy of composition that exploits writing as a philosophy" (130). In other words, he argues for a classroom in which, as he says quoting Henry Miller, "there is no progress: there is perpetual movement, displacement, which is circular, spiral, endless" (130). For Covino, then, writing is "informed by associational thinking, a repertory of harlequin changes, by the resolution that resolution itself is anathema" (130). Or, similar to my epigraph that quotes Covino, writers write to see what happens. In Covino's pedagogy, uncertainty, though not necessarily profitable or fashionable, "provokes the investigation of possibilities beyond one's stock response; uncertainty necessarily sends us into conversation with other ideas and people" (130).

Obviously, Covino's pedagogy is an attempt to import postmodernist thought directly into composition classroom practice. It is the sort of practice that postmodernism calls for in that, as Ward notes, "in Covino's class, knowledge is understood to unfold as 'drama of people and ideas' and students are expected to participate in this inventive process" (137). As Covino defines it in *Forms of Wondering: A Dialogue on Writing, for Writers*, his pedagogy revolves around the notion of interactive dialogue. He writes in the introduction to this first-year writing textbook:

What you have here is very different from other textbooks, mainly because it is written as a *dialogue*. . . . Reading this

> book means participating in the dialogue, taking part—in your
> own mind and through your own writing and talks with your
> classmates—in the *exploration* that writing and reading and
> serious discussion can provide us, and in the *community* that
> we create whenever we add other voices to our own. (xv)

In order to achieve this dialogue, Covino creates "characters," or
voices, that represent aspects of himself and that he labels Covino the
Sophist, Covino the Expediter, Covino the Epistemologist, Covino
the Writing Teacher, Covino the TV Watcher, Covino the Radical,
Covino the Administrator, and Covino the Textbook Writer. In a dialogic (or perhaps polylogic) drama, these characters engage in a
discussion of questions, conflict, misunderstanding, and many other
aspects of writing. In other words, Covino offers a text that is not
only self-reflexive in design, but is postmodern in that it allows students to engage in a dialogue about writing while recognizing the
multifaceted ways in which an individual comes to writing. Covino
encourages recognition of the role of dialogue in writing not only
through his script but also through the assignments which the text
offers: he encourages students to respond to his "assignments" in
dialogic writing just as he has offered the assignments to them. This
he claims will equip students to better engage in future communicative acts.

Several scholars have criticized Covino's pedagogy. Ward's critique, for instance, notes Covino's failure to "question the classroom
setting as a scene of writing" and that student writing only "remains
practice for some future coming to be, a conceptual status that the
postmodern classroom would like to deconstruct" (144). Moreover,
Ward argues that in Covino's pedagogy "the scene of writing remains
traditionally Hegelian and, in many ways, monologic in that students never engage in dialogue with any actual others, and, hence,
their writing never gains the status of communication, understood as
communicating meaning in order to have an effect in the world"
(144).

While Ward and others critique pedagogical applications of facets
of postmodernism, one is tempted to respond "So what?" to many
such criticisms. It seems that critics of postmodern pedagogy, be they
opposed to parts or all of a pedogical application, frequently desire a
panacea pedagogy. But postmodernism does not allow for a pedagogy to evolve that accounts for every practical need a critic might
call for. So, the development of postmodern theory may aid pedagogy; it may, in fact, serve particular pedagogical developments, but

in order for postmodernism and composition pedagogy to best serve each other, there cannot be a totalizing postmodern pedagogy, nor can pedagogy be the sole purpose for postmodern development. Post-modernism, like other theories that find their way into composition, in order to be of benefit, must develop beyond classroom applica-tions. As Ward concedes, "Despite Covino's major attempt to construct a postmodernist pedagogy, the most important work in postmodernism and composition has not been in the development of pedagogy, but, rather, in scholarship" (144).

PERCEIVING THEORY
IN COMPOSITION

In his response to *Contending with Words*, Sosnoski, like Covino and Phelps, attempts to translate what influence post-modern and poststructuralist theories actually have on classroom practices. Since each of the essays in this collection makes an attempt to tie theory and practice together in a dialectical relationship, Sos-noski has no problem discussing classroom issues such as assignments, syllabi, course designs, teacher-student relationships, and so on in relation to the contributed essays. For instance, he argues that the position Bizzell takes in her essay "Marxist Ideas in Composition Studies" would possibly lead to a course design that is based on the works of Freire, Fredric Jameson, and Henry Giroux and that serves to critique hegemonic structures in discursive prac-tices. Within this critique, Sosnoski suggests that Bizzell's course would encourage students to "become critical members of their dis-ciplines. Their critiques would embody not only an impulse to resist this discipline but also a utopian impulse" (205). While I don't believe that Bizzell's pedagogy would turn to Freire as much as Sos-noski suggests, he does identifiy the central aspect of what could be derived as Bizzell's pedagogy: critique-based practice. Likewise, Sos-noski derives critique-based pedagogies from the works of Herzberg, John Clifford, and Susan Jarratt. One goal of postmodern theory, and hence postmodern pedagogy, is to resist, critique, and disrupt hege-monic structures, and Sosnoski finds in Bizzell's work a precise link between her theory and a potential practice. However, he then attempts to suggest course designs based on every author's contri-bution to this collection. Sosnoski, like many other compositionists, exhibits a compulsion to locate theoretical endeavor in practical application. Certainly, we can see a pragmatic need to do so, particularly in a text directed toward practitioners, whether they play the double role of theorists as well or not. However, the implication of Sosnoski's (and perhaps the field's) need always to return to practice as a final application of theory suggests an underlying mood of the profession.

3

Postprocess Theory and the Pedagogical Imperative

"The world does not speak. Only we do. The world can,
once we have programmed ourselves with a language,
cause us to hold beliefs. But it cannot propose a language
for us to speak. Only human beings can do that."
—*Richard Rorty,* Contingency, Irony, and Solidarity

"Let the words be yours, I'm done with mine."
— *The Grateful Dead, "Cassidy"*

Within composition's theory/practice debates, many
scholars have criticized the recent explosion of theoretical work as not
answering the "real" problems that composition instructors face in
their daily grade-and-grind lives.[1] Often, compositionists assess the
value of a particular theory based on what immediate impact it has on
classroom practice. Lynn Worsham has labeled—and I have borrowed
for my title—this need to ground theory in practice a "pedagogical
imperative" and the "will to pedagogy" (96). While many (including I
myself) have argued against this position, it is my intention to show
how one particular line of theoretical inquiry—postprocess theory—
has been intruded upon by composition's pedagogical imperative in
ways that have not produced workable pedagogies and have, in fact,
denied major facets both of postprocess theories and theoretical pursuit in general.

Let me begin by briefly recapping the position from which I operate. Within composition studies, there are theoretical pursuits which
extend beyond classroom application. That is to say, composition
has become an intellectual discipline in its own right, and in order
for scholars in composition and rhetoric to responsibly pursue
inquiry into all facets of discourse study, particular theories, lines of
thought, inquiries may not necessarily lead to immediate classroom
application. That is *not* to say that these pursuits are of no value in
composition; on the contrary, certain theoretical pursuits may lead to

a better understanding of the operations of discourse without leading to immediate pedagogical development. For instance, theorists who speculate about the function of language or attempt to make sense of philosophies of language push us toward a more thorough understanding of discourse. Specifically, I am referring to language philosophers such as Richard Rorty, Donald Davidson, and Thomas Kent. While I find the work of these scholars particularly intriguing and insightful, it is this same kind of scholarship which invites much criticism from those uninterested in composition theory beyond classroom application.

Understandably, many in composition and rhetoric have resisted the discipline's move toward theoretical modes of inquiry; after all, composition has traditionally been viewed as merely a service to the university—a service that involves teaching students "the basics." It does not include engaging in intellectual inquiry. Even respected compositionists such as Maxine Hairston, past chair of the Conference on College Composition and Communication, have criticized composition from turning away from its roots: teaching. So it seems logical, under these pretenses, that compositionists be angered at the theoretical road down which the discipline has turned. It even seems, at first, in the best interests of the field to determine value of theoretical pursuit based on immediate classroom application. However, prejudices that suggest that theoretical pursuit is of little value to the discipline or that wholesale translation of composition theory into practice is necessary deny a responsibility to intellectual endeavor, to the field, to students, and to ourselves as professionals.

Such is the case with postprocess theory. Because this theoretical endeavor is somewhat new to composition, some have criticized it as not being the sort of theory the field needs. That is, it does not answer questions of "real" classroom issues. Even those who see the classroom potential of postprocess theory have too hastily fallen into the pedagogical imperative and seek to create pedagogies from theories we are just beginning to discuss. It seems that the pedagogical imperative demands that for a theory to be of value in composition it must immediately effect classroom practice, so even those compositionists who do not shun postprocess theory because of what it suggests about discourse—about the relationships of students and teachers— feel obligated to bring it to the classroom because many believe that to be the testing ground for composition theory. Often, however, such wholesale translation from theory to practice denies particular theories their revolutionary potential, discredits certain theories before they have been thoroughly explored, and, in effect, neutralizes the innovations individual theories offer the field in favor of already inscribed assumptions and practices. Again, such is the case with postprocess theory.

NEW PRAGMATISM AND CONTINGENCIES OF LANGUAGE

Richard Rorty, in works such as *Philosophy and the Mirror of Nature* and *Contingency, Irony, and Solidarity*—particularly, the essay "The Contingency of Language"—argues against foundationalist concepts of knowledge in an attempt to redefine contemporary analytic philosophy. Rorty wishes to move philosophy away from understanding "knowledge" and "mind" as the "natural" subjects of philosophy toward an "epistemological behaviorism" that recognizes these concepts as historical terms. As he puts it, "About two hundred years ago, the idea that truth was made rather than found began to take hold of the imagination of Europe" (*Contingency* 3). Through his critique of contemporary philosophical inquiry, Rorty examines language and the "metaphor of conversation." As John Trimbur and Mara Holt explain, "For Rorty, representations of knowledge, mind, truth, and rationality result from a figurative language that has held philosophers captive, a set of unacknowledged metaphors that picture the mind as a glassy essence equipped with a mental mirror to reflect reality and an inner eye to contemplate these reflections" (71). In other words, he views the epistemological traditions of Western philosophy as an attempt to find foundational, secure, and perhaps permanent truths and knowledges when, instead, we should regard knowledge and truth as social practices, matters bound up in the metaphor of language. For Rorty, philosophy—and, in turn, all other disciplines—cannot escape its own discourse. There is no way for a discipline to free itself from its language and "get at" the thought expressed through the discourse; there is no way to shake free from the contingencies of a discipline's vocabulary.

In order to recognize the role language plays in how philosophical inquiry and, by extension, all inquiry is shaped, Rorty examines the ways in which philosophy has traditionally been viewed as a discipline. He writes that

Some philosophers have remained faithful to the Enlightenment and have continued to identify themselves with the cause of science. They see the old struggle between science and religion, reason and unreason, as still going on, having now taken the form of a struggle between reason and all those forces within culture which think of truth as made rather than found. These philosophers take science as the paradigmatic human activity, and they insist that natural science discovers truth rather than makes it. They regard "making truth" as a merely metaphorical, and thoroughly misleading, phrase. (*Contingency* 3)

Trimbur and Holt explain that the image of philosophy that Rorty defines

Takes shape in the modern period with Kant's effort to define philosophy as a foundational discipline. For Kant, philosophy is distinct from science, demarcated by its special task of establishing a theory of knowledge upon which science and other forms of inquiry may rest. While the empirical disciplines can produce knowledge, it is given to philosophy alone to ask what makes knowledge possible in the first place, to adjudicate knowledge claims, to act as tribunal of reason with the other disciplines under its jurisdiction. (73)

Yet Rorty argues that Kant and Hegel "went only halfway in their repudiation of the idea that truth is 'out there.' They were willing to view the world of empirical science as a made world—to see matter as constructed by mind, or as consisting in mind insufficiently conscious of its own mental character" (*Contingency* 4). He argues that "we need to make a distinction between the claim that the world is out there and the claim that truth is out there":

To say that the world is out there, that it is not our creation, is to say, with common sense, that most things in space and time are the effects of causes which do not include human mental states. To say that truth is not out there is simply to say that where there are no sentences there is no truth, that sentences are elements of human languages, and that human languages are human creations. (*Contingency* 4–5)

In other words, as I have quoted him in my epigraph, Rorty argues that we view the world through our language; the world does not tell us which language to use. He points out, however, that the "realization that the world does not tell us what language games to play should not, however, lead us to say that a decision about which to play is arbitrary, nor that it is the expression of something deep within us" (*Contingency* 6). So, for Rorty, how we engage philosophical inquiry, all inquiry, is based on nothing more than which language, which vocabularies, we choose to use. For instance, Rorty turns to Kuhn's speculations about paradigm shifts in scientific inquiry. Kuhn argues that scientists create new ways of thinking about a particular phenomenon not because they have discovered some greater truth about it; rather, by creating new ways to talk about that phenomenon, the perceived truth about it shifts to be commonly understood in terms of the new model created by the new language.

Rorty posits that philosophical inquiry traditionally would have a difficult time finding its identity without theories of knowledge or in a time when scientific thought dominated Western thinking. Instead, by locating philosophy in historical contexts, Rorty attempts to break down barriers between philosophy and rhetoric. He seeks to historicize philosophy in ways that force us to recognize that philosophy is defined not by methods but by vocabularies. In doing so, he claims that there are no foundational, universal means by which to identify truth and knowledge but that we must recognize philosophy as a narrative, one which simply represents past views of the discipline only in ways current language is able to—not definitive ways.[2] Consequently, Rorty wants to help "readers, or society as a whole, break free from outworn vocabularies and attitudes" (*Mirror* 12).

Contending that philosophy has been unaware of the metaphors it creates, Rorty posits that it is "metaphors rather than statements" which "determine most of our philosophical convictions" (*Mirror* 12). He argues that rather than seeking out accurate relationships between language and the world, we need to reexamine how we view language. Trimbur and Holt suggest that "We should talk about language as neither a privileged object of inquiry nor a transparent medium of representation that can bring us into privileged relationship to reality. Rather we should think of language as an endless circulating discourse that can bring us into relationship to other speakers, other metaphors, other discourse" (77). For Rorty, then, the fluctuating nature of language contests traditional philosophical inquiry's search for universal knowledge, for what he calls a "final vocabulary," a master vocabulary.

Turning to Wittgenstein, Heidegger, and Dewey, Rorty argues against Western philosophy's aspiration to achieve consensus for what qualifies as rationality. He disagrees with what he identifies as philosophy's attempt to "impose a norm of discourse upon speakers" (Trimbur and Holt 78). Instead, Rorty argues for hermeneutics as a method to resist and subvert philosophy's goal of unidiscourse. In other words, Rorty is not attempting to "correct" traditional philosophical thought; he would argue that there is no "correct" view of philosophy, only more appropriate metaphors for inquiry. Rorty employs hermeneutics to get beyond traditional epistemological, philosophical views in order to better recognize relationships "between various discourses as those of strands in a possible conversation, a conversation which presupposes no disciplinary matrix which unites the speakers, but where the hope of agreement is never lost as long as the conversation lasts" (*Mirror* 318).

Perhaps the clearest way to understand Rorty's notion of language is to draw on yet another metaphor that Rorty uses. Rorty comes to his theories of discourse by way of Donald Davidson, whose work I will discuss shortly. Drawing on Davidson's Wittgensteinian notion of language as an alternative tool, Rorty presents the metaphor of "language-as-tool." He argues that frequently we don't have the right tools to complete a task effectively. So, new tools are invented, old ones altered to fit, and the need for specific tools is sometimes stumbled upon while working through the job. Rorty suggests that language operates much like a new tool: when a tool is not sufficient to complete a task, a new one is developed; or when an old tool is not as effective as a new one, it is put aside. He also suggests that sometimes we may stumble onto a tool and have no idea what to do with it yet; like many of the gifts we may recieve from second cousins, we just have to ask, "Well, it looks neat, but what does it do?" Rorty argues that new vocabularies evolve out of necessity as new ways of discussing, of perceiving, phenomena are needed. Rorty's "language-as-tool" is illustrated by several episodes of the television program *MASH* that relied on new-tool-development as plot. In such episodes, Hawkeye and company would face a surgical situation that they could not handle with the tools available to them. Rather than pass the problem on to the "hospital in Seoul," because surely the wounded soldier would die in route, the medical team always set out to invent a tool that would do the job. Over the years the various characters managed to invent several varieties of clamps, surgical tools, an incubator, and even a portable dialysis machine. Each of these new tools allowed the unit to expand its repertoire of battle-side surgery tools—or, as Rorty would describe it, their surgical discourse shifted, and the new tools altered the "knowledge" they shared.

Rorty explains that new vocabularies are not always "created" because of a need, nor are they necessarily stumbled upon as one might find in a kitchen-supply store a great new utensil that revolutionizes how one makes omelettes on Sunday mornings. Rather, vocabularies might shift from what Rorty terms "normal discourse"—those uses of language that are consistent with the "conventional" way of perceiving and describing a subject—to newer discourses that have not yet achieved consensus within the discourse community. Normal discourse occurs when a discourse community reaches consensus as to what language presents a good explanation of how a phenomenon is understood; in other words, normal discourse is the language that in a particular historical context offers sufficient explanation of a phenomenon. When, as Kuhn has explained, a new vocabulary about a phenomenon evolves that in some way contradicts the normal discourse and thus presents a new way of perceiving and understanding the subject, this new language is considered to be abnormal discourse. This is not to say that any language that is different from consensus language is abnormal; rather, abnormal discourse must have the potential to become normal discourse and alter a discourse community's knowledge. Rorty argues that normal discourse becomes such "not because we have discovered something about 'the nature of human knowledge' but simply because when a practice was continued long enough the conventions which make it possible . . . are relatively easy to isolate" (*Mirror* 321). On the other hand, Rorty explains abnormal discourse as occurring when "someone joins in the discourse who is ignorant of these conventions or sets them aside" (*Mirror* 320).

Yet, when Rorty is confronted with critique of what role normal and abnormal discourse plays in first-year writing courses, he is quick to relegate first-year composition courses to a service position. When Gary Olson, in his 1989 interview with Rorty, asks if first-year composition should teach students to strive to create abnormal discourse, Rorty is adamant as to the function of beginning composition courses: "I think the idea of freshman English, mostly, is just to get them to write complete sentences, get the commas in the right place, and stuff like that—the stuff we would like to think the high schools do and, in fact, they don't" (232). He goes on to say that he thinks of "abnormal discourse as a gift of God rather than anything anybody gets educated for or into" (234). I bring this up now not to discredit Rorty or his theories of language, but to recognize that even those scholars whose work provides the theoretical basis on which current theoretical and practical pursuits—knowledge making—are put

forward have difficulty letting go of the traditional view of the composition classroom even when what seems to be the core of their
argument may suggest otherwise.

Rorty identifies knowledge making in two distinct ways. First, he
says that knowledge can be recognized as evolving from conflict
between that which wants to know (the subject) and the phenomenon
about which there is inquiry. This grows from the traditional idea that
the more a phenomenon is prodded, confronted, studied, the more
likely we can get closer to the "truth" about that phenomenon. That
is, the more likely we are to search for and find a "true reality" about
that thing—a search for foundational knowledge. Rorty argues that
this type of knowledge leaves no room for contestation or conversation—the second way knowledge is made. If we understand
knowledge to be an evolving product of conversation, "Certainty will
be a matter of conversation between persons rather than a matter of
interaction with non-human reality" (*Mirror* 157). This can be a quite
unsettling way to view knowledge making for some, and it draws
much criticism and attention from those who see anti-foundationalism as a threatening way of looking at knowledge making. Trimbur
and Holt point out that Rorty's position can be

> Unsettling because it disqualifies traditional habits of thought
> that picture a legitimatizing source of knowledge outside
> ourselves and our discourses. The irreducibility of Rortyean
> conversation may in fact elicit a kind of linguistic claustro-
> phobia. To imagine human culture and the quest for
> knowledge as a conversation between persons instead of con-
> frontation with reality may appear to lock us in a "prison of
> language," a hermeneutic circle that offers no release, no
> standpoint to get outside our discursive practices in order
> to show how things really are. (81)

In other words, Rorty, while explaining knowledge making as relative
to discourse and conversation, is critiqued as limiting knowledge to
the confines of language. Rorty, however, contends that this feeling of
entrapment is problematic only to those who wish to be outside the
conversation. He argues that this desire to exist beyond the conversation is one of the primary illusions of Western philosophical
inquiry:

> As long as we think that there is some relation called "fitting
> the world" or "expressing the real nature of the self" which

can be possessed or lacked by vocabularies-as-wholes, we shall continue the traditional philosophical search for criterion to tell us which vocabularies have this desirable feature. But if we could ever become reconciled to the idea that most of reality is indifferent to our descriptions of it, and that the human self is created by the use of a vocabulary rather than being adequately or inadequately expressed in a vocabulary, then we should at least have assimilated what was true in the Romantic idea that truth is made rather than found. What is true about this claim is just that *languages* are made rather than found, and that truth is a property of linguistic entities, of sentences. (*Contingency* 7)

For Rorty, we cannot escape discourse, nor can we use discourse to escape from the world since discourse is ubiquitous; it defines our world and, thus, cannot be left behind. Instead, as Trimbur and Holt explain, "the task we face is that of learning to live in a world without foundations, in a world of ungrounded, floating discourses, where conversation is its own sufficient aim and justification" (81). And while Rorty perceives truth as being created by vocabularies, by conversations, he does not deny that truth cannot be found "out there": "to say that we should drop the idea of truth as out there waiting to be discovered is not to say that we have discovered that, out there, there is no truth" (*Contingency* 8).

ALTERNATIVE TOOLS AND TRIANGULATION

Perhaps, in order to grasp Rorty's work better—particularly, its implications for composition—it should be seen in light of how it has been influenced by Donald Davidson's scholarship and how, in turn, Davidson's work has directly influenced the thinking of certain compositionists. In the introduction to his 1993 interview with Donald Davidson, Kent introduces an audience of compositionists to Davidson in this way:

Donald Davidson is an analytic philosopher in the tradition of Wittgenstein and Quine, and his formulations of action, truth, and communicative interaction have generated considerable debate in philosophical circles. In the areas of composition studies and rhetoric, however, Davidson is relatively unknown; he possesses neither the name recognition nor the influence of other contemporary philosophers of language to whom we regularly look for support and guidance. . . . Although Davidson does not occupy a conspicuous place in composition and rhetoric's pantheon of heroes, his ideas have nonetheless influenced—albeit indirectly—the study of writing. Davidson has entered our lives primarily through his influence of Richard Rorty, who, in turn, stands along with Thomas Kuhn as one of the two most prominent progenitors of social constructionist theory. (1)

Rorty turns to Davidson in his discussions of the contingencies of language because, as he says, Davidson is the philosopher who has done the most to explore this area. Rorty writes that Davidson's "treatment of truth ties in with his treatment of language learning and of metaphor to form the first systematic treatment of language which breaks *completely* with the notion of language as something which can be adequate or inadequate to the world or to the self" (*Contingency* 10). It is within this break that Davidson contests the traditional understanding of language as *medium*. Kent explains that for Davidson

If language does not mediate between us and the world, as Davidson claims, and if we cease to imagine that a split exists between an inner world of thought and feeling and an outer world of objects and events, as Davidson advocates, then nothing exists "out there" or "in here" that will serve as an epistemological foundation for either a theory of meaning or a theory of truth; all we have to authorize our utterances are other utterances. (1)

We can hear the echoes of this in Rorty's claim that only sentences can be true. Rorty argues that Davidson rejects the view of language as medium because if we continue to see language as medium we stay grounded in subject-object perceptions of the world and our inquiries about language are relegated to questions such as, does the mediation "between the self and reality get them together or keep them apart? Should we see the medium primarily as a medium of expression—of articulating what lies deep within the self? Or should we see it as primarily a medium of representation—showing the self what lies outside?" (*Contingency* 11).

Rorty argues that Davidson helps us find a way off of the "see-saw" between these romantic views of language and similar questions that could be asked of language as moralistic. Davidson does not regard language as a medium for expression or representation. Rather, like Wittgenstein, Davidson views language as a tool and alternative languages as alternative tools. Davidson, thus, seeks to avoid reducible vocabularies, all-encompassing vocabularies, and questions about vocabularies that lead to reductionism. Instead, Davidson would direct us to ask questions about how our vocabularies influence our uses of other vocabularies—questions that inquire as to the effectiveness and efficiency of our tools.

Davidson is, by his own claim, an anti-foundationalist; he has "departed from foundationalism completely" and claims that he "never went for foundationalism," that he "was never taken by any version of it." It is for him, a mistake ("Language" 5). Yet, he does not deny that "foundationalism is alive," though he would "like to think it isn't well" ("Language" 5). Davidson's anti-foundational position is even more clearly clarified through his theories of language and inquires as to how language affects communication, knowledge making, and truth. In both his theories of "communicative interaction" and "triangulation," Davidson argues that the ways in which subjects experience the world cannot be conceptualized or schematized. He argues in "A Nice Derangement of Epitaphs" that this inability to grab hold of *how* we experience is equally prominent in *how* we communicate. He posits that no encompassing foundation allows us to make sense of sentences, claiming that "there is no such thing as a language, not if language is anything like what many philosophers and linguists have supposed" ("Nice" 446).

It has long been believed that in order for language to function as a method of communication some framework or shared scheme must be in place to keep an interpretive community together—similar to what Kuhn calls a "paradigm" and Davidson labels a "conceptual scheme." This paradigm allows members of an interpretive community to approach discourse similarly. Because each conceptual scheme is unique to that interpretive community and, in turn, each community speaks a different language, this suggests that each interpretive community shapes its own language. However, Davidson argues that interpretive communities do not create their own language but, rather, that language creates the perception of what is an "interpretive community." Davidson understands that it is impossible for anyone to shed conceptual schemes in order to identify those of another (*Inquiries* 184–85). This is not to say that there is *no* conceptual scheme. Instead, Davidson posits that even within an interpretive community individuals possess different conceptual schemes. This notion leads to a conceptual relativism that then questions the inter-translatability of language. At the same time, Davidson contends that there is no evidence that conceptual schemes are shared. Hence, there can be no place from which we can speak that answers to another's knowledge making. As Kent puts it, "such a claim must mean that no neutral ground exists on which we can stand to make true statements about the world. . . . We always speak from within some interpretive community, so we cannot step outside our own community to inter-pret what members of other communities experience or believe" ("Interpretation" 43). Yet, despite his turn to highly contextualized notions of communication, Davidson recognizes that even though conceptual schema cannot translate between individuals in an inter-pretive community, to some degree they must translate. That is, as Kent explains:

> We cannot live in different worlds and speak incommensurate languages if we recognize that someone is failing to commu-nicate. All this problem means is that we have not employed a hermeneutic strategy that functions well enough to help us interpret what someone else desires us to understand. The upshot of Davidson's critique is clear: the claim that incom-mensurate interpretive communities exist is incoherent. (44)

How then does Davidson view the operation of language interpreta-tion to inform effective communication? In "A Nice Derangement of Epitaphs," he turns to the example of the malapropism to show how he sees the interpretive process unfolding. He argues that someone playing the role of interpreter in a communicative situation comes to an "occasion of utterance armed with a theory that tells him (or so he believes) what an arbitrary utterance of the speaker means" ("Nice" 440). As the communicative situation unfolds, the participant playing the role of speaker says something with the intention that the inter-preter will be able to interpret it. However, Davidson argues, "In fact this way is not provided for in the interpreter's theory. But the speaker is nevertheless understood; the interpreter adjusts his theory so that it yields the speaker's intended interpretation" ("Nice" 440). Davidson refers to this as the speaker "getting away with it." He writes that the speaker may or may not recognize that "he has got away with any-thing; the interpreter may or may not know that the speaker intended to get away with anything. What is common to the cases is that the speaker expects to be, and is, interpreted as the speaker intended although the interpreter did not have a correct theory in advance" ("Nice" 440). He tells us that "We all get away with it all the time; understanding the speech of others depends on it" ("Nice" 440). For Davidson, then, both speakers and listeners are forced to continually shift their hermeneutic strategies of interpretation—a strategy Kent has termed "hermeneutic guessing" and participating in a "hermeneutic dance."

Davidson more thoroughly describes the operations of communicative interaction through two theories he labels "prior theory" and "passing theory": "For the hearer, the prior theory expresses how he is prepared in advance to interpret an utterance of the speaker, while passing theory is how he *does* interpret the utterance. For the speaker, the prior theory is what he *believes* the interpreter's prior theory to be, while his passing theory is the theory he *intends* the interpreter to use" ("Nice" 442). According to Davidson, then, in any communicative interaction, both participants are required to adjust their hermeneutic strategies and both participate in the situation by speculating as to what each other knows and does not know in order to successfully complete the interpretation. By engaging in the hermeneutic strategy of interpretation, by employing the passing theory, we engage in a process of what Davidson calls "triangulation."

Davidson argues that, in order for a communicative situation to play out, three sorts of knowledge are brought to the scenario: knowledge of our own minds, knowledge of others' minds, and knowledge of what we share in the world with the other participants in the communicative situation. In other words, Davidson creates a triangle in which the shared knowledges about each other and the shared world leads to how we construct our hermeneutic strategies in communication.

In this assessment of how communication operates—and, in turn, in Rorty's philosophy of language—little distinction is made between written communication and any other communicative scenario. Davidson privileges spoken discourse over written discourse. However, we can certainly see from the number of times discussions of Rorty, and indirectly of Davidson as well, make way into composition scholarship that their theories have implications in how we see written discourse. It would be very difficult to construct a pedagogy based on arbitrary vocabularies, hermeneutic guessing, triangulation, and abnormal discourse. In fact, these theories question considerably the possibility of whether written discourse *can* be taught. And yet, these philosophies of language, these solely theoretical discussions, find a place in theoretical knowledge that holds the potential to at some time impact our practical needs. In fact, these theories are benificial now; they teach us different ways to think about discourse, about writing. And at the same time, we can learn more about discourse, and perhaps these theories may one day teach us enough to offer specific changes in our pedagogies.

Part of my argument in favor of theoretical pursuit grows from a tradition of *theory* that has greatly influenced ways of thinking. As I argue in Chapter One, theoretical knowledge has played a crucial role in epistemological development and cannot be abandoned in composition in promotion of solely practical pursuits. To demonstrate this further, and to parallel some of the theories being put forward in the philosophy of discourse, I would like to draw momentarily on an example from the sciences. When Guglielmo (William) Marconi began his experiments involving electromagnetic waves, there was absolutely no practical use for his work. He worked exclusively in terms of theory. As he progressed in theoretical speculation, his work was apparently of no more use than to delight his cousins by "magically" moving compass needles from across the room. In fact, as he continued his work, Augusto Righi, his professor at the university in Bologna, discouraged Marconi from delving into the mystery of the invisible waves. However, as he furthered his pursuit and combined his efforts with discoveries made by Morse and Bell, Marconi slowly learned to send short waves over short distances and then longer waves over long areas of space. In time, Marconi's theoretical speculations about radio waves became the basis for contemporary electronic communication.

So, like Marconi, the theoretical endeavors put forward by Rorty and Davidson perhaps stand to directly influence composition practice at some time. But until their works are thoroughly investigated in terms of composition and composition pedagogy, they will remain as theory that helps inform us about aspects of discourse that do not directly tie to our classroom pedagogies. Scholars have already begun to explore the implications that Davidson and Rorty have more directly on composition. Kent, for instance, has employed Davidson and Rorty to critique the paradigms composition employs.

POST-PROCESS THEORY

Perhaps some of the most important current scholarship in composition related to such theories is that put forward by Kent. While drawing on Jean François Lyotard, Rorty, and occasionally Derrida, Kent relies heavily upon Davidson's philosophies. He argues that communicative interaction relies on fluctuating hermeneutic strategies. Hence, he says that Davidson (as well as Derrida) suggests that "neither writing nor reading can be taught as systemic process" ("Paralogic" 25). Labeled "postprocess" composition, this model seems to be at the forefront of the direction in which composition scholarship is moving and, therefore, receives a good deal of critical attention. More and more, compositionists seem to be concerned with the theories that attempt to expound upon the nature of discourse analysis and production.

In several of his major works, Kent posits that traditionally discourse production and interpretation have been regarded as a "logico-systemic process and then codified according to certain ontological categories like Kantian schemata, discursive models, or discourse communities, and these categories, in turn, are employed in classrooms to teach writing and reading" ("Paralogic" 24). Within composition, he says, the three dominant logico-systemic approaches are the expressivist, the empirical, and the social constructionist. He contends that although these three approaches appear different, "they nonetheless share one common foundational assumption. They assume that discourse production and analysis can be reduced to systemic processes and then taught in classrooms in some codified manner" ("Paralogic" 25). Kent argues that if we instead think of discourse production/interpretation as fluctuating and requiring hermeneutic guessing strategies, then we must rethink "our basic assumptions both about the acts of writing and reading and about the rhetorical tradition from which our current theories of writing and reading are derived" ("Paralogic" 25). Here, Kent's sentiment is clear: if we are to value these language theories, we must reconsider not only our practices, but how we have come to these practices by way of theory as well.

Kent begins his critique of current composition paradigms by introducing compositionists to Davidson's theories of communicative situations. He argues that the idea of discourse communities, which compositionists have come to rely on, is an invalid concept in light of what Davidson teaches us about discourse:

> A so-called "discourse community" possesses little ontological validity in that no concrete language convention can be isolated that holds it together. Members of discourse communities cannot be said to share a specific language convention or a set of language conventions that enable them to produce

discourse; at best, they share only a common hermeneutic strategy that enables them to *begin* to produce discourse that they believe will be comprehended by others, a process that cannot be codified or described exactly. What we share with our neighbors within a discourse community—if such a community exists at all—is a shared interpretive theory that helps us begin to guess about the interpretation others might give our discourse. ("Paralogic" 26)

For Kent, the paralogic hermeneutic strategies involved in discourse production and interpretation have strong implications for how we teach writing and reading. He posits that we need to "rethink our rhetorical tradition, especially the genealogy of rhetoric as a discipline," and we need to "develop radically different pedagogical approaches to teaching reading and writing" ("Paralogic" 33).[3]

Taking into account the fluctuating and shifting nature of communication, Kent argues that we cannot teach students to produce or analyze discourse since "We cannot in any systemic way reduce discourse to metalanguage that describes itself" since "discourse production and analysis refute systemization" ("Paralogic" 35). He posits that since we cannot match our strategies of hermeneutics with anyone else's

We ceaselessly shift ground in our guesses about how others may be interpreting our language code, and because of the paralogic skill and background know-how required to shift ground, we cannot codify our interpretive acts and then arrange them in any sort of systemic metalanguage. (35)

Hence, according to Kent, we have to recognize that textbooks cannot adequately represent the operations of discourse and its analysis and production. More importantly, he acknowledges "the impossibility of teaching writing and critical reading as an epistemologically centered body-of-knowledge," since writing and reading teachers generally assume that they do teach a "body-of-knowledge," one "that is organized by a predictive theory" ("Paralogic" 35). In other words, it seems as though most teachers assume that discourse functions in relation to the world in some predictable way—that there can be no totalizing theory of discourse, that not even an amalgam of a variety of theories can explain how discourse operates. However, it is not to say, as Kent argues, that there can be no metalanguage to discuss variable elements of discourse—punctuation, grammar, and so on—although Kent says that mastery of these elements does not necessitate that one will be able to produce effective discourse. Kent posits that when we try to teach writing or reading processes we run into the same difficulty in that the systemic meta-languages we employ to describe the process presupposes a certain amount of background knowledge. In other words, the metalanguage breaks the confines of discourse, and so its "truth" is no greater than that of the process it seeks to describe. Kent explains that

> Many pedagogical approaches to composition derive their legitimation from the claim that writing consists of a recursive process where the writer moves back and forth among a series of steps . . . the pedagogy provides a metalanguage that explains how to invent, how to select, how to organize, and so on (see LeFevre). With this process approach to writing instruction, however, we assume that the writer can discover, in some predictable way, what it is she wants to say and how to say it: we mistakenly assume that a fit, link, or convention exists between the different hermeneutic strategies employed by both the writer and the reader. ("Paralogic" 36)

With this in mind, Kent adamantly argues that process pedagogies, in composition and elsewhere, "go out the window" ("Paralogic" 37). He surmises that if we are to understand that the acts of producing discourse and analyzing discourse are no different, cannot be detached from the interpretive strategies of hermeneutic guessing, then "no course can teach the acts of either reading or writing. Because all of our process-oriented composition and literature courses assume that a student posseses certain background know-how, even if the know-how represents only knowledge of a natural language, these writing and reading courses can only modify this background knowledge; they cannot teach a student *how* to employ it" ("Paralogic" 37). The only way for students to learn *how* to imple-ment their background knowledge is to engage in interpretive strategies and become more adept at playing the hermeneutic guess-ing game. For Kent, then, classrooms do not become a place where teachers inform students about discourse, but rather teachers become another voice in the dialogue that helps them become acquainted with their interpretive strategies.

In addition to radically calling into question the practicalities of process pedagogy, Kent's paralogic hermeneutics holds some power-ful ramifications for social constructionism. As I mentioned earlier,

Kent is quick to point out that any system of codification of ontological categories—such as those we use to classify expressivism, empiricism, social constructionism, and so on—assumes a foundational system of classification. Kent argues that

> *If no codifiable link exists that connects the sign to its effect in the world, then no formal system of rhetorical analysis— no metalanguage—can be formulated that will account for the tropological use of language.* Any rhetorical theory, linguistic theory, or literary theory that attempts to explain the relation between metaphor and metonomy or attempts to describe the uses of language . . . must posit or, at least, must presuppose a conventional link between the sign (or the sentence) and its effects in the world. ("Beyond" 504–05)

He goes on to explain that "many of our most influential theories of discourse analysis can explain satisfactorily neither the nature of language nor how the effects of language are produced" ("Beyond" 505). Claiming that with no way to codify connections between signs and their effects on the world there can be no logico-systemic account of discourse production, Kent offers a radical critique of social constructionism:

> The social semiotic approach assumes that a conventional link exists between the members of different discourse communities, and meanings as well as knowledges are grounded in socially constructed conventions; therefore the sign (or the sentence) may be interpreted only through the sign's conventional effect in these different discourse communities. If no convention can be found to link the sign (or the sentence) to its effect in the world, then the presuppositional foundation that supports . . . these theoretical approaches to discourse production is seriously undermined if not destroyed entirely. (504)

In other words, Kent questions the foundational aspects on which even social constructionist theory relies, and he calls into question the very notion of "discourse community" which has become central to social constructionism.

According to Kent, social constructionism's concepts of discourse fall into a spectrum of formulations of community with one end of the spectrum represented as "thick" and the other end as "thin." The thick formulation, he explains, "understands community to be a system of social conventions that may be isolated and then codified" ("Idea" 425). Or, as Irene Ward explains it, discourse communities "are envisioned as determinate systems that constitute frameworks from which the members of these communities understand the world" (151). The thin formulation, on the other hand, understands community as a "chorus of polyphonous voices" in which participants belong to many overlapping and fluctuating discourse communities at once ("Idea" 425).

Like Davidson's conceptual schemes, social constructionism's discourse communities function in that

> In the thick formulation, the social conventions that create the communities in which we live also constitute the framework we employ in order to survey the passing scene. In the thin formulation, we may survey the passing scene only by listening to and joining in the different and often contradictory voices that make up what Bakhtin calls the heteroglossia of community life. In both cases, however, our knowledge of others and of the world always will be relative to the particular conceptual schemes or communities in which we exist. ("Idea" 426)

So Kent argues that "from the social constructionist perspective, knowing the world means knowing a particular conceptual scheme, and knowledge is something we acquire by learning and internalizing the normative conventions that constitute our conceptual schemes" ("Idea" 428). Hence, Kent sees the idea of discourse community, of incommensurate conceptual schemes, as a self-refuting idea. He explains:

> If members of different discourse communities speak, as Bruffee says, "quite different languages," then we could never understand them at all. Discourse communities cannot be incommensurate, for if they were, we should not even recognize them as being discourse communities. Therefore, the thick formulation of incommensurate discourse communities makes no sense. Of course, the thin formulation of commensurate discourse communities makes no sense either, for if each discourse community is commensurate with every other one, we no longer need the concept of a discourse community. ("Idea" 428)

Furthermore, Kent argues, if, as social constructionism sees it, there is a split between the mind and the world, "how can we ever be sure that we know the minds of others or that we can know with any certainty anything at all about the world?" ("Idea" 428). He also charges social constructionists with an impassable relativism. He asserts that in social constructionism "meaning and knowledge are relative to a conceptual scheme, and since conceptual schemes in the form of social norms obviously change from place to place and from time to time, nothing exists to authorize one set of practices or beliefs over another set" ("Idea" 429).

In Kent's model, then, communicative action moves composition studies beyond cognitive, expressive, and social understandings of how language functions toward a fluctuating paralogic system of hermeneutic guessing. He argues that our view of discourse production, of reading and writing, and of how we come to understand and teach reading and writing have been limited by our relegating them to linear, recursive *processes*. For Kent, reading and writing are not codifiable processes. We cannot teach how discourse operates; only by engaging in communication can we begin to hone our hermeneutic strategies. Such views of discourse, of pedagogy, of communication force us to consider the implications in the classroom even if those proposing these ideas spend little or no time developing pedagogical "applications."

POSTPROCESS AND THE COMPOSITION CLASSROOM

Several attempts both to bring Kent's theories to the classroom or to critique the impossibilities of doing so have emerged following Kent's forwarding of paralogic hermeneutical composition theories. Obviously, Kent's radical relativism suggests that "teaching" writing or reading is a misguided concept. However, as I have discussed, both composition as a field and the institution of the university are not as willing to concede that composition cannot be taught. Even Richard Rorty, whose own scholarship supports these ideas of communication, is not willing to let go of the traditional perception of composition courses as a place where students are taught to "get the commas in the right place" (Olson, "Rorty" 232). Then, for many compositionists who see theory as useless unless it informs pedagogy, how we bring these philosophies of language to the classroom defines their value. However, the theories of Rorty, Kent, and Davidson do not necessarily have to be constructed into actual, operable pedagogies to be of value. The new ways in which these theories help us see discourse undeniably influence how we *think about* discourse, about our pedagogies, and about how our students learn. This is certainly enough to warrant these theories as valuable. However, since many compositionists would still wish to see tangible classroom application, a few scholars have begun to discuss ways in which these theories impact the classroom.

In his 1993 presentation "Dialogue and Post-Process Theory in Advanced Composition" at the Conference on College Composition and Communication convention, Raul Sanchez initiated a conversation regarding ways that Kent's postprocess theories can influence composition classroom practices. Sanchez argues that if we are to incorporate Kent's work into our classroom practices, our teaching will need to undergo fundamental changes, particularly "how we envision our relationship to our students." Drawing examples from writing textbooks' introductions, Sanchez details how the writing process becomes the content of writing courses. He contends that discourse is too complex to fit the process model: "the process-oriented classroom is often an unproblematized environment, a 'content course' in the worst sense of the word, where the instructor acts as a dispenser of knowledge and the student is an empty vessel." Like Kent, Sanchez finds fault with the process model for presenting the mind as a "conscious and independent force that only has to manage its internal chaos effectively and organize its pre-existing content." Sanchez concludes that process pedagogy does have one important advantage: it is relatively simple to teach. Instructors can clearly and unproblematically present a body of knowledge and evaluate students' performance based on their ability to absorb and master it.[4] In other words, process pedagogy requires that students merely learn to repeat the information that has been dispensed to them—information, Sanchez claims, that is often just the teacher's version of the writing process itself.

Sanchez offers a "postpedagogical" alternative to this traditional model, since even if we believe we cannot really teach writing, we can't just leave students on their own to engage in discursive activity.[5] Instead, he sees the role of the teacher as a collaborator and guiding force as students engage in hermeneutic activity. This procedure will help students encounter more hermeneutic strategies than they might encounter on their own. This postpedagogy calls for a more complex view of the student-teacher relationship: "one where the instructor creates and to some extent embodies the text." In this scenario, writing instructors assume a role of master to the student/apprentice. Both teachers and students participate in a hierarchical relationship that is established on the instructor's understanding of the paralogic nature of discourse and the operations of hermeneutic activity. Learning, then, comes from "hands-on" experiences with someone who already understands discourse—someone who can share that insight with students or suggest how students' own discourses can blend with or create distance between other discourses.

Sanchez's Kentian pedagogy suggests an emphasis on individualized instruction and a reevaluation of student-teacher relationships. He claims that the need for lectures and traditional class discussions would be significantly reduced and that classroom time would be better spent focusing on individual or small-group needs. In this model, since there is no longer a "text," instructors must depend on their ability to analyze and produce discourse; the "text" is then created through teacher-student interaction and discourse. Instructors must learn to be "acutely aware of each student's 'progress,' because in the absence of the process paradigm the student has no other authoritative voice on which to depend."

While Sanchez's pedagogy certainly attempts to bring postprocess theory to practical application, it is wrought with problems, both practical as well as theoretical ones. His effort to bring theory to the classroom is admirable, and while paralogic hermeneutics may inform pedagogy and the way we think about discourse, this is one example of a theory that cannot necessarily be "translated" wholesale into a pedagogy.[6]

Obviously, Sanchez's pedagogy presents a problem of logistics in his teacher-student model. It becomes impossible to offer one-on-one attention to all students. Surely, most writing program administrators would be forced to dismiss this approach as soon as they became responsible for providing and budgeting each student with a mentor, and traditional single-teacher classrooms simply cannot provide this type of attention on a regular basis. Granted, most composition instructors would argue that their pedagogies might fall somewhere between the two models. Most of us are eager to make "good use" of classroom time but are also willing, if not eager, to offer individual time to students. It is from this understanding that students' needs to encounter discourse on an individual level and the classroom need of providing for many students are met. Hence, pedagogies that involve conferences and small-group work along with classroom pedagogies seem to be a legitimate compromise that allows for the introduction of some of the facets of postprocess theory into the classroom.

In addition to these pedagogical logistics, Sanchez's pedagogy denies a crucial aspect of Kent's understanding of discourse production and analysis. If we understand meaning and truth to be created through discourse, and if in order to engage in discourse effectively, we must hone our hermeneutic guessing strategies, then Sanchez's pedagogy is limiting. By confining students' learning about discourse to a two-participant model—mentor and apprentice—students learn only one model of discourse. Postprocess theory lends itself to allowing students to become aware of their own subject positions; by encouraging individuals to become adept at strategically altering their hermeneutic skills in each communicative scenario, individuals become attuned to multiple schemas that impact how they encounter dialogue and, in turn, how they encounter the world. Mentor-apprentice strategies seem more limiting than pedagogies that encourage students to hammer out their conceptual schemas through contact with multiple other participants in discourse and give students the opportunity to discover their positions in discourse, in the world.

Perhaps the most relevant criticism of Sanchez's pedagogy, though, is his definition of the role teachers play. By placing instructors in mentor positions and suggesting that they would "already understand discourse production and analyses," Sanchez contradicts a major facet of the theories from which he draws. Kent clearly argues that we can never "understand" discourse operations and that we can never establish a metalanguage through which to explain those operations to others. Sanchez's mentors, then, must be language wizards who exist beyond the confines of discourse and who are capable of passing their insight on to those of us trapped in the realm of sentences. Kent, Rorty, and Davidson would all see this as an impossible position to hold.

While Sanchez's pedagogy is problematic, his insight into ways in which postprocess theory can *possibly* impact pedagogies is helpful. Though he carries it to an extreme, his ideas about individualized attention for students seem beneficial and perhaps can effect ways in which to think about conferencing and small-group work. Also, he certainly calls into question ways in which we think about both instructors and students and forces us to reevaluate how we "administer" knowledge to our students rather than participate in learning with them.

Like Sanchez, Ward finds postprocess theories beneficial in redefining pedagogies. Ward turns to Kent to identify ways in which postprocess theory comes to composition classrooms. Unlike Sanchez, she is less willing to redesign classroom structures. Ward acknowledges that Kent only vaguely discusses how his theories *could* be applied to classrooms, yet he describes a classroom in which students enter "into specific dialogic and therefore hermeneutic interactions with others' interpretive strategies" ("Paralogic" 37). Because, as he argues, "to enable a student to employ her background knowledge, an instructor, at best, can offer only advice, and as an adviser, the instructor must relinquish the traditional role of lawgiver and assume the very different role of collaborator" ("Paralogic" 37).

Ward then turns to Sanchez's pedagogy to envision ways in which these roles *might* be established. However, Ward is cautious not to provide the kinds of definitive implementations of postprocess pedagogy that Sanchez does. It seems that Ward is conscious of the important role that postprocess theory plays in our continuing attempt to understand discourse, yet she is less apt to translate those theories into viable pedagogies just yet. This administration of the theory/practice interaction at first seems scrupulously responsible. Yet, while I am glad to see how Ward handles this integration, I am bothered by the inherent perception that in order for her discussion of these theories to be of any value it must at some point lead to practical application. In fact, Ward turns to Sanchez's discussion of postprocess pedagogy in what seems to be a "way out" of her theoretical discussion.

Very little has been written about this sort of postprocess pedagogy. Perhaps Kent's own glossing of classroom application should serve as an indication that these theories, while informative about the nature of discourse, are not necessarily practice-oriented theories, a recognition which, of course, puts us at an awkward crossroads. While I applaud Sanchez for attempting to further discussion about the importance of postprocess pedagogy and theory, I am confused by the perception that is put forth by him, Ward, and even Kent that in order for these theories to be worth discussing they must inform our practice. Certainly, we are compositionists, and we find value in talking about composition and how what we talk about influences how we teach composition. But these discussions of postprocess theory have only recently begun. Our eagerness to immediately gratify ourselves with pedagogies that we can *do* with this new theory seems hasty and to some extent, as the problems these pedagogies present themselves, frivolous. I fear that both Kent and Ward fall prey to disciplinary prejudice that their discussions would be met with calls of "So what? What's that got to do with us?" if they didn't address practice in some way—even in half-hearted addendums. At times, it seems as if Kent has begun pedagogical discussions not because they seemed applicable to his arguments but because he was asked to do so by an editor who wanted the article to be more "appropriate" for a composition journal; these discussions seem less thought out than the rest of his work. Ward also seems to tack on her section about post-process pedagogy as an afterthought. Of course, some may argue that we are compositionists and talking about composition classrooms is what we do; it is how we define ourselves. This criticism calls into question my interrogation as to why we *must* relate these conversations to practice. But, as I have argued earlier, this desire to ground the identity of composition studies ultimately in classroom practices relegates us to a service position within academia.

When compositionists bring theories like those put forward by Rorty and Davidson or others like Kent into composition, there is an inherent prejudice that these theories must have practical application. At times, many compositionists shy away from theories like post-process theory since without immediate practical appeal they lose value. Even those scholars from whom we draw our theories seem eager to dismiss the value of theory in light of application. Rorty claims to be suspicious of theoretical justification of practice. When Olson suggests that compositionists such as Kenneth A. Bruffee have been influenced by his work to develop collaborative pedagogies, Rorty shrugs off the idea by saying, "I guess if the way Bruffee does it works, fine" ("Conversation" 230). And when questioned directly as to how he sees theory informing practice, he responds, "Well, obviously they play back and forth, but in as concrete a case as this it seems to me that you can just see whether a pedagogic experiment succeeds; if it doesn't, that may leave the theory intact or it may not, but the thing to do is find out whether it actually works" ("Conversation" 230). Bruffee, too, in response to the interview, takes offense at distinctions made about theory and practice:

> Rorty is not a "theorist." Neither am I. Social construction is not a theory. It is a way of talking, a language, a vernacular. Least of all is social construction a "theoretical rationale for collaborative learning." It is a way of describing collaborative learning. The theory-practice dichotomy is one of the notions endemic to foundational thought that makes it so constraining and so thoroughly obsolete. (236)

Bruffee tells us that Rorty is correct in arguing that there is a play between theory and practice but that he is also right to say that the primary goal is to "find out whether it actually works" (236).

Rorty and Bruffee are not alone in privileging classroom practice, particularly in composition classrooms. Davidson also begins to shift his position when asked specifically about both writing and classroom practices. When Kent asks Davidson how his theories apply specifically to written discourse, Davidson seems to privilege spoken discourse. He argues that there are many different cases in writing scenarios that engage the writer-audience relationship in a variety of ways. However, he argues that there must be a presupposed understanding of a shared body of knowledge since the interaction between reader and writer usually does not allow for direct communication between the two ("Conversation" 14–15). When asked to discuss pedagogy in light of his work, Davidson seems less interested in pursuing pedagogical discussions. He says, "there's a sense in which I don't think of myself primarily as instructing or, at least, passing along information" ("Conversation" 14). Again, the split between theory and practice is emphasized.

POSTPROCESS COMPOSITION AND ANTI-FOUNDATIONAL FEAR

Several times in this chapter and those that precede it, I have mentioned that part of the anti-theoretical stance comes from a fear of the anti-foundational positions of many contemporary theories. Postprocess theory, for instance, posits a relativism that suggests that even in the most trivial communicative interaction we can never really be sure that meaning is transmitted exactly as a communicant intended it. This, in turn, holds dark implications for the big issues like truth. Postprocess theory, then, might seem to undermine many of the ideals that draw compositionists to the field and the same ideals that dominate other bodies of composition theory.

As we have begun to find new ways to talk about written discourse, we have attributed great power to it. We have begun to realize how discourse can marginalize groups, empower other groups, and in fact we frequently depict it as the defining force of our world. Compositionists have begun to discuss composition classrooms not as a place where students come to learn to "get it right" (although the university and even some compositionists may wish to relegate us to that role) but as a place where students learn to engage their world, to become critically conscious, to find their voices in the multitude of others that make up language. Postprocess theory for many, though, stands to undermine these ideals. Certainly, we can see the anxiety that a theory that implies that truths dissolve and that we cannot necessarily "teach" writing would cause for those of us who have invested not only our idealism but also our livelihood in a field where we believed we could help "better" our students.

To some extent, composition has relied on foundationalism to promote many of its ideals—foundationalism, that is, as Stanley Fish defines it: "any attempt to ground inquiry and communication in something more firm and stable than mere belief or unexamined practice" (*Doing* 342). We want to be able to say that the expressivist model is right, that the cognitivist model is right, or that the social construction model is right. We want to be able to rely on "things"— things like, as David W. Smit points out,

> The "real world," the referential nature of language, and human rationality and intersubjectivity. After all, most of us live and act as if the real world exists and that we can depend on it: we never seriously doubt that in the foresee-able future the sun will continue to come up in the east, and we depend on the fact that our homes will still be there when we come back from vacation—or if they are not, we assume that there will be clear signs as to why they are not: ashes, for example. (35)

As compositionists, we operate similarly: we want to be able to go to our classrooms, teach writing, see our students engage discourse; and we want to be able to identify that when we are finished our students are not only better writers—that is, closer to mastering discourse—but also better people, and if they are not, we want clear signs as to why.

But a postprocess anti-foundational approach to discourse calls into question our ability to do those things, questions, in fact, that teaching writing can even be *done*. Anti-foundationalism offers questions of

> Fact, truth, correctness, validity, and clarity [that] can neither be posed nor answered in reference to some extracontextual, ahistorical, nonsituational reality, or rule, or law, or value; rather, Anti-foundationalism asserts, all of these matters are intelligible and debatable only within the precincts of the contexts or situations or paradigms or communities that give them their local and changeable shape. (Fish, *Doing* 344)

But at the same time that anti-foundationalism shakes the ground on which many of us find satisfaction in composition, it has also helped us promote some of the very ideals which many see as threatening. Compositionists such as Patricia Bizzell, Lester Faigley, Kent, and Smit have engaged anti-foundationalism and composition in ways that reinforce idealistic goals of helping our students become more than "better writers."[7] Granted, these scholars' works are targeted by those who resist the anti-foundational position, they are targeted mainly due to misunderstanding. If we are to peruse any major composition journal's recent issues, we are likely to find any number of articles which engage anti-foundationalism and composition—both theoretically and practically.[8] In fact, Smit argues that "scholars in Composition and Rhetoric are overwhelmingly antifoundationalist" (36). While I am not sure I agree wholeheartedly with Smit's sweeping optimism, it is apparent that anti-foundationalism does play a large role in contemporary composition studies.

4

FEMINIST THEORY AND
ITS INTERACTION WITH
COMPOSITION PEDAGOGY

"Breaking old chains and traditional modes of writing is
never without its dangers."
— *Clara Junker, "Clara Junker Responds"*

"The split between feminist theory and practice is
artificial."
— *Joy S. Ritchie, "Confronting the
'Essential' Problem: Reconnecting Feminist
Theory and Pedagogy"*

Feminist composition theory has become a critically
important area in composition scholarship, despite the fact that feminism has been regarded with what Rosi Braidotti calls the "mentality
of the special issue" rather than as an integral part of theory.[1] Feminist compositionists such as Marilyn Cooper, Elizabeth Flynn, Susan
Jarratt, Clara Junker, Susan Miller, and Lynn Worsham have established feminism as a legitimate concern in composition scholarship.[2]
These scholars attempt to identify unique ways in which women
compose, and they look to make direct ties between the multiplicity
of feminist theories and composition theory and pedagogy. Yet the
numbers of competing feminisms and the differing ways in which
they influence composition scholarship create inherent tensions in
adapting these theories to composition pedagogies—especially for
male compositionists.

Rosmarie Tong points out that there are many different types of
feminisms: cultural, liberal, radical, psychoanalytic, socialist, marxist, and postmodern, to name a few. Compositionists find that there
are a number of tensions created in trying to determine which aspects
of the many competing feminisms are most beneficial to composition.
In other words, it is difficult for compositionists to conceptualize
what "feminist composition theory" is or can be. This is not necessarily a problem unique to composition, but it certainly does affect

feminist composition scholarship. This multiplicity of theoretical stances is problematic in finding ways to import feminism into the classroom and forces us to inquire how issues of gender and language construction might influence composition theory and pedagogy.

VALIDATING FEMINIST THEORY

In her landmark essay, "Composing as a Woman," Flynn describes how current thinking in composition can be seen as a "feminization" of how we previously understood composition. Flynn argues that in a way compositionists have shifted their understanding of written discourse and "replace[d] the figure of the authoritative father with an image of a nurturing mother" (423), and we have turned from accepting the final form of a text as a product produced by established writers with a gift for words to seeing writing as a long process that involves working with words. This image derives from a concern for the growth and maturity of students, and Flynn identifies the influence the "foremothers" of composition have had in perpetuating this image—compositionists such as "Janet Emig, Mina Shaughnessy, Ann Berthoff, Win Horner, Maxine Hairston, Shirley Heath, Nancy Martin, Linda Flower, Andrea Lunsford, Sondra Perl, Nancy Sommers, Marion Crowhurst, Lisa Ede" (424). At the same time, Flynn acknowledges that male compositionists have also had a role in the feminization of the field, and she is quick to recognize James Britton's contributions. Flynn's recognition of Britton here is crucial. While she is obviously interested in discussing the role women have played in the field's development, her recognition of male contribution to what has been criticized as a male-dominated field suggests an understanding that both women and men must participate in the search for composition studies' identity and the development of its theories.

Flynn recognizes that feminist inquiry and composition's search for knowledge are similar and suggests that this is perhaps why a good deal of important feminist scholarship emerges from the same departments that house composition studies.[3] However, Flynn also points out that "feminist studies and composition studies have not engaged each other in a serious or systematic way" (425). She criticizes the major journals for not including discussions of feminist issues often enough and the Conference on College Composition and Communication for its infrequent inclusion of convention panels on feminist issues (Flynn does note the 1988 convention but only as an exception). Certainly, Flynn's argument has been heard, and the major journals now more regularly include articles pertaining to feminist issues; for instance, the *Journal of Advanced Composition*'s 1990 special issue on gender, culture, and ideology was the first of several special issues related to gender published by various composition journals. And a quick glance at the programs for the 1993 CCCC convention in San Diego, the 1994 convention in Nashville, and the 1995 convention in Washington, D.C., reveals that more than twenty-five panels, presentations, and special interest groups at each addressed either feminist or gender issues. While these numbers do not suggest that we have reached an equilibrium, they do indicate that compositionists have recognized the importance of feminism and have begun to explore more thoroughly the interaction between it and composition studies.

Flynn argues that part of what feminism and composition need to explore is "just what it means to compose as a woman" (425). She posits that due to an imbalance in the social order in which men have traditionally dominated women, feminist inquiry—research and theory—"emphasizes that males and females differ in their developmental processes and in their interactions with others" (425). She further explains the feminist position as an understanding that men have

> chronicled our historical narratives and defined our fields of inquiry. Women's perspectives have been suppressed, silenced, marginalized, written out of what counts as authoritative knowledge. Difference is erased in a desire to universalize. Men become the standard against which women are judged. (425)

Flynn argues that within composition feminist inquiry would question the role of difference and dominance in written language. She asks, "Do males and females compose differently? Do they acquire language in different ways? Do research methods and research samples in composition studies reflect a male bias?" (425).

Flynn does not attempt to answer these questions or solve these problems in her essay; rather, she is concerned with discussing how feminist research on theoretical approaches to gender difference "may be used in examining student writing, thus suggesting directions that a feminist investigation of composition might take" (425). Flynn—like other compositionists examining other theories—looks for an immediate validation of feminist theory through practical application. She seems to justify feminist theory not through the importance of the questions it asks about discourse and gender difference but through ways she sees it as useful in approaching student writing. Flynn surveys recent feminist theory in order to devise a way that it "may be used."

Flynn contends that her application of feminist theory to particular student essays "is not meant to demonstrate the validity of feminist scholarship but to suggest, instead, that questions raised by feminist researchers and theorists do have a bearing on composition studies and should be pursued" (431). However, like other theorists who feel obligated to ground theory in composition pedagogy, Flynn *is* looking for validation. She seems to want to prove that feminist theory *does* have a place in composition and, in order to do so, must surrender to the idea that for any theory to be of value to compositionists it must have practical application. Feminist theory has certainly altered the ways in which we think about discourse and patriarchy's dominance of it; feminist theory has also helped composition pedagogy evolve in many useful ways. Yet, Flynn—both a compositionist and a feminist—falls prey to the understanding of composition studies as a solely practice-oriented field. While I applaud the concern for even offering a section called "Pedagogical Strategies" that derives from specific theories, I am concerned with the desire for validation—an impulse she tries to deny (432). Like other scholars who attempt to incorporate outside theories into composition, feminist scholars in composition face problems of validation and value. They also face the seemingly difficult task of bringing theories to a patriarchal discourse that in most cases seek to overturn, alter, or disrupt that discourse.

There is an apparent tension that grows from trying to bring feminism—and its agenda for disruption—to composition and its sometimes constrictive nature. By creating a need for validation through pedagogy—that is, a need to *do* feminism in the classroom—the strain put between feminism and composition at first seems to weaken feminist theory and to allow composition to maintain its patriarchal grip over which theories are to be *used* and how they will be used. Again, composition's prejudice for confirmation by practice seems to neutralize feminist thinking. However, while this tension appears to be—and frequently receives criticism for being—detrimental to the engagement between feminism and composition, feminist theory has certainly altered how we think about composition. Composition's continued search for identity has been greatly influenced by the tensions that occur when composition and feminist theory come together. Perhaps in this instance, tension is more beneficial to composition than it is to feminism—that is, ultimately composition will benefit more from these tensions—but as with other theories that come to composition, one of our goals as compositionists is to better understand written discourse. Feminist theory pushes us in that direction.

DISRUPTING COMPOSITION

As I have discussed, composition is a discipline often relegated solely to the domain of *teaching* written discourse, particularly academic discourse. Frequently, feminism in its various incarnations seeks to disrupt this discourse. For instance, the French feminist notion of *écriture féminine* calls for women to "write themselves."[4] Typically translated as "feminine writing" or "writing the body," *écriture féminine* is writing that is understood to be feminine writing. "Writing the body" means rejecting traditional discourse, which is thoroughly male inscribed and phallogocentric, and attempting to write from a uniquely feminine perspective, substituting the biology of the female for that of the male. Hélène Cixous explains that "woman" must not write within the confines of patriarchal discourse "in her inevitable struggle against conventional man," and she speaks of a "universal woman subject who must bring women to their senses and to their meaning in history" (245). She argues that

> Woman must write her self; must write about women and bring women to writing, from which they have been driven away as violently as from their bodies—for the same reasons, by the same law, with the same fatal goal. Woman must put herself into the text—as into the world and into history—by her own movement. (245)

For Cixous, part of feminine writing is a disruption of patriarchal conventions. She is adamant that the future no longer be determined by past standards, and while she cannot deny the effects of the past, she refuses to reinforce them by repeating them. Her vision of *écriture féminine* is a struggle against patriarchy. For Cixous, "woman must write woman. And man, man" (247).

Cixous posits that "men have committed the greatest crime against women" by turning women against themselves (248). She

calls for women to break free from male confines and argues that
discourse, that writing in particular, has been defined by a male
libidinal culture. She contends that history, the history of writing, has
been demarcated by a "self-admiring, self-stimulating, self-congratu-
latory phallocentrism" (249). Yet, by writing the self, women, Cixous
argues, will learn to control their histories, their subjectivity in history, by returning to the body which has been confiscated from them
by phallogocentric histories.

Cixous's language is that of revolution; she cries for liberation.
Women, she claims, have been "reduced to being the servant of the
militant male" (250). Yet, through writing, woman has the opportunity of "*seizing* the occasion to *speak*, hence shattering entry into
history, which has always been based on her *suppression*" (250).
Writing awakens woman to her self, to her voice; "a woman without
a body, dumb, blind, can't possibly be a good fighter":

> It is by writing, from and toward women, and by taking up the
> challenge of speech which has been governed by the phallus,
> that women will confirm women in a place other than that
> which is reserved in and by the symbolic, that is, in a place
> other than silence. They shouldn't be conned into accepting a
> domain which is the margin or the harem. (250, 251)

Cixous's arguments against the phallogocentric nature of discourse, of writing, of history call into question ways in which we
have understood writing. In turn, *écriture féminine* forces us to question our approaches to composition studies and to our pedagogies.
Yet the subversive nature of *écriture féminine* conflicts with much of
composition's established identity. While many of the theories that
have been imported into composition studies have been beneficial in
overturning old conceptions of the field and of how discourse operates, *écriture féminine*'s revolutionary language appears threatening
to many in composition.

Since many compositionists—and the academy in general—seem
to have decided that composition is a matter of teaching students
how to "get it right"—how to, in fact, operate within a phallogocentric discourse as though academic discourse were the universally
correct discourse—many resist *écriture féminine*'s invasion into composition. However, for those who are willing to see *écriture féminine*
as possessing potential for understanding discourse in new ways,
several questions come to the fore: How does one recognize *écriture
féminine*? How does a field that is traditionally phallogocentric

encourage feminine writing without appropriating, weakening, or subverting that writing through a well-inscribed phallogocentrism? And, similar to questions which are asked of other theories in composition, what is the accountability of this feminist theory? Yet, for feminist compositionists, questions of *écriture féminine*'s effect on composition seem less crucial than questions of composition's effect on *écriture féminine*.

In "Writing against Writing: The Predicament of *Ecriture Féminine* in Composition Studies," Worsham makes the argument that *écriture féminine* cannot be imported into the writing classroom to work alongside academic discourse. She argues that if composition were to make any sustained contact with *écriture féminine*, one of two things would happen:

> either composition would neutralize the radical potential of *écriture féminine* in an effort to appropriate it to serve the current aims of the profession and, beyond this, the university, or *écriture féminine* would cast such suspicion on the whole enterprise of composition studies as an accomplice of phallocentrism that composition would be transformed beyond recognition. (93–94)

For Worsham, composition is a discipline that "defines itself largely as a discourse community whose positive task it is to teach academic discourse(s)" (82). Because she views the field in terms of the identity many have inscribed on composition, she identifies a conflict between the mission of *écriture féminine* and the mission of composition, since *écriture féminine* is

> a language "event" that, in its more accessible moments, unleashes a damning critique and denunciation of academic discourse as the instrument par excellence of phallocentrism. (82)

In other words, the tension between *écriture féminine* and composition would require either the complete redefinition of the discipline of composition studies or the neutralization of *écriture féminine*.

Worsham suggests that perhaps composition has not been a deterrent to *écriture féminine*—or has accepted those few articles which import *écriture féminine* into composition—since composition may wish to seem receptive simply "to display its cultural capital by contending with the newest intellectual fashions, and French feminism is certainly *haute couture*" (83). Yet, at the same time, she recognizes the oversimplification of this argument. For Worsham, *écriture féminine* "is one of the most dramatic developments in recent writing theory and pedagogy" (83). Here, her distinction between theory *and* practice is evident: in order for *écriture féminine* to be valuable to composition studies, it must exist as theory and practice. *Ecriture féminine* is, for Worsham, of use in both aspects "not only because it may reformulate our notion of literacy and its consequences but also because it could produce a crisis in composition's self-understanding" (83). Hence, in Worsham's eyes, part of the benefit of bringing *écriture féminine* to composition is its ability to encourage a reexamination of—and perhaps a dramatic shift in—the very notion of composition.

Ecriture féminine is a new language, a new way to speak, to write—a way which is inherently at odds with established phallogocentric methods. Worsham points out that scholars from many fields, then, set out to find ways to identify and codify its features so that it can be recognized as a system of discourse. There is an expectation that, as with other languages, other forms of discourse, scholars should be able to identify a single theory or group of related theories that holds the discourse together—that there are, in fact, ways to distinguish concretely what constitutes "feminine writing" and to some extent what it means to be "woman." There is a (phallocentric) assumption that *écriture féminine* can be identified as "an object of knowledge and a repository of truth" (84). Yet *écriture féminine* is "typically found lacking, fraught with contradictions, riddled with (theoretical) inconsistencies, and short on concrete strategies for changing the material conditions of everyday women's lives" (84). In other words, *écriture féminine* resists the systematic and codifiable categorization that traditional phallocentric understanding of "knowledge" attempts to impose—resists, in fact, traditional knowledge making in composition studies. Composition has not deterred feminisms from entering into scholarly conversations; however, Worsham argues that previous attempts to bring French feminist thought to composition have neutralized its "radical potential" and at the same time have taught us much about our "ideological investments of writing theory and pedagogy" (84).

Since, as Worsham argues, *écriture féminine* "resists every effort to make it an object of knowledge and a spectacle for the gaze of epistemologists," it, in many ways, cannot be brought to the university. It cannot be theorized; it cannot be objectified. "It cannot become the object of research and scholarship; it cannot become the basis for a pedagogy" (92). Hence, those attempts to do so—to import *écriture féminine* into composition studies—cannot leave *écriture féminine* to its agenda; instead, it becomes appropriated and loses its radical edge. Worsham posits that, because of this neutralizing, *écriture féminine* "does not want to be brought, from its position on the margin of official culture, into the university. It is more likely to decimate, not invent or reinvent, the university and its discourses" (93).

It is clear, then, that French feminist theories of *écriture féminine*

cannot be freely imported into the writing classroom to work alongside academic discourse toward the goal of literacy—that is, to the extent that literacy and the literate mind are governed by the epistemoligical attitude and its positioning of the speaker or writer in a phallic position of mastery over discourse. (Worsham 93)

While scholars of literacy (I will discuss this term more clearly in Chapter Five) attempt to identify a consensus in communication and knowledge making, *écriture féminine* seeks to disrupt phallogocentric notions of consensus discourse and mastery over such discourse. Worsham posits that *écriture féminine*

laughs in defiance of this narrowly political project for improving the human condition. This laughter is not that of an anarchist or nihilist. It should suggest instead that literacy itself is a regime of meaning to be interrogated regarding its power to recuperate the power of those already in a position to order and give meaning to the social world. (93)

Despite the radical edge that French feminism could potentially bring both to composition and to the university, Worsham concedes that previous attempts to bring French feminism into the university have resulted not in radical upheaval of composition studies but in the neutering of French feminist theory. Worsham turns to two articles that attempt to bring French feminism to composition and that, in doing so, received substantial criticism. Both Robert de Beaugrand's "In Search of Feminist Discourse: The 'Difficult' Case of Luce Irigaray" and Junker's "Writing (with) Cixous" investigate the interaction between French feminist theory and composition studies, and, in turn, are criticized for appropriating and neutralizing particular aspects of feminisms.

NEUTRALIZING THEORY

In his "In Search of Feminist Discourse," de Beaugrande acknowledges that feminist thought has begun to have great
impact on English studies, yet he sees no "consensus about the
detailed consequences that we should expect" from these influences
(253). He argues that since much feminist theory posits that issues of
gender and language run deeper than simple pronoun problems, "an
acute dilemma arises. The English profession is a plausible institution for elaborating critiques of discourse and bringing the results to
the awareness of the general public. But, if the bias of discourse runs
so deep, how can we hope to find a neutral discourse for our own critiques?" (253). In other words, de Beaugrande wants to know how we
can escape a patriarchal discourse long enough to offer a nonpatriar-
chal critique of that discourse.

In asking this critical question, de Beaugrande points out that
feminism seeks to put forth and use radically different types of discourse.[5] He warns that we must be cautious of how we judge these
new communicative discourses, since we judge them from a limited,
preordained position influenced by phallogocentric language. Noting
an alliance between feminist methods and deconstructive methods of
discourse analysis, he argues that

> If conventional discourse is indeed pervaded by the premise
> of male bias, then one promising way to move in another
> direction is to appropriate a mode of discourse that continu-
> ally undercuts its own premises. Though the bias is not
> ultimately removed, it at least becomes problematic instead
> of being permitted to work smoothly. Stripped of its surrep-
> titious status, the bias appears increasingly obtrusive,
> self-exaggerated, despotic. (255)

Yet he also sees a risk in applying techniques of feminism as a
critique of discourse. De Beaugrand suggests that feminism may be
vulnerable to four types of misrepresentation. One position derives
from those who do not understand feminisms' radical, experimental
discourse(s) and concludes that "feminists don't know what they
want" (255–56). A second argument contends that radical feminism
creates superfluous problems that stand in the way of discourse's
progress. The third criticism attacks feminists "for not having established a space wherein they can define their own discourse for once
and for all, freed of all involvement in male bias" (256). The fourth

criticism—an extension of the third, and most often raised by "political feminists"—argues that feminist discourse "fails to generate concrete analyses that could promote interventions in the praxis of social discourse" (256).

What de Beaugrande sees, then, as the crux of the matter for critics of discourse—deconstructionists as well as feminists—is a series of questions regarding the relationship between language and the "world":

> Does the relation between language and the "world" retain enough leeway to allow a substantive remodeling of our consciousness? Can we get free enough from language to watch it at work and introduce a new balance? Can we deregulate the functioning of discourse so that its limits could be differently drawn? Can we deconstruct our entrenched conceptions, and the discourses that presuppose them, to the point where a genuinely non-aligned system of discourse might enable a free and commensurate communication among all humans, be they women or men? (257)

In order to answer these questions, de Beaugrande argues that we must first assess the size of the task, and he posits that experimental feminist discourse offers a space in which to make such an assessment. He warns, however, that feminist discourses, like other discourses that have sought to disrupt dominant discursive systems, have frequently been misunderstood or absorbed and rendered neutral. In order to examine this space, de Beaugrande turns to a reading of Luce Irigaray's two best-known books translated into English: *Speculum of the Other Woman* and *This Sex Which Is Not One*. He says of his reading of Irigaray that

> To get beyond my own reactions to her discourse by not filtering it through my own paraphrase, I shall attempt to work through some of her main points by arranging and quoting her own words. In this way, I may be able to capture enough of her voice to convey some of the intricate, often cyclical movement she prefers over the usual forward march of argumentative and philosophical discourse. (258)

Though he recognizes his reading of Irigaray presents a different agenda from that of her original text, de Beaugrande feels that the risk taken in such a reading is worth it "if we can set the projects of experimental feminism into a more appropriate perspective than the commonplace polemics of confrontation, accusation, and misrepresentation" (258). Herein lies the neutralizing power that de Beaugrande imposes on feminism and the position from which he earns much criticism for this essay.

Some feminists argue that men cannot write the same feminism as women and that de Beaugrande, by not acknowledging his masculine position in approaching Irigaray's work, appropriates feminist discourse. By not conceding his limited (male) vision of the feminist discourse he uses, de Beaugrande takes the position that as a male he can produce feminist discourse the same as if a woman had written his article. The question of his situatedness is called into play. Donna Haraway explains in "Situated Knowledges: The Science Question in Feminism and the Privilege of Partial Perspectives" that traditional notions of objectivity have generally assumed the "unmarked positions of Man and white" (188). The traditional "objective" position, according to Haraway, is that of an authority who stands outside of a phenomenon and "objectively" reports what is observed. Haraway has labeled this perspective the "god-trick," and she argues against this limited vision. De Beaugrande appropriates feminism for his use by not acknowledging his role as situated knower, as a male who is using feminist discourse. Instead, he uses his "god-trick" vision to report how feminist discourse operates as though his perspective offers a clear (objective?) view of the truth about feminist discourse. Here, the issue is one of situatedness, which he fails to acknowledge. Many feminists critique de Beaugrande for assuming a position in which he attempts to report feminism from an objective position. In a postmodern world, we have come to recognize that knowledge—including feminist perspectives—cannot be reported objectively. De Beaugrande, however, is seen as attempting to be objective with feminist theory—attempting, that is, to appropriate feminism as a discourse males can *do*, possess, and master.

Similarly, Worsham notes that de Beaugrande's essay operates as a servant of "the machine of hegemony working to neutralize the radical potential of *Ecriture Féminine*" (94). She points out that de Beaugrande does not expressly set out to defuse the radical edge of French feminism, but Worsham says that beyond the conscious intention we must be aware that essays like de Beaugrande's, "in their desire to give French feminism meaning within composition, unwittingly contain and neutralize it within an ideological space that it resists and refuses" (94). Worsham argues that de Beaugrande makes a conscious effort to avoid creating a metalanguage about Irigaray's work by instead working her words into his essay. He says he wants to "get beyond my own reactions to her discourse by not filtering it through my own paraphrase" (258). Worsham contends that his concern is to show that he is on the "right" side of her discourse rather than to react to it. However, Worsham reads his arrangement and selection of quotes not as a means to affiliate his discourse with Irigaray's, but as "the culmination of a process of (in)filtration and political interpretation" (98).

At the same time, Worsham questions de Beaugrande's use of the word *difficult* in his title. She claims that we are to understand his choice of the word and his highlighting it in quotation marks as calling "to mind a negative (male) stereotype of women" (98). She suggests that the title—while perhaps identifying de Beaugrande's sense of humor—certainly "calls attention to the fact that the interpreter chooses to play the part of analyst explaining (curing?) the case of the difficult, the enigmatic female (discourse)" (98).

De Beaugrande claims that even though feminism is beginning to have effect in the profession we still "find no widespread consensus about the detailed consequences that we should expect" and that feminism seeks "experimental forms of discourse that attempt to propose and practice a radically different mode of communication" (253). Worsham focuses on these points and argues that these are precisely the standards that seek to neutralize *écriture féminine*—communication and consensus:

> Consensus, commensurability, communication, "non-aligned" discourse—these are the old dreams of the Enlightenment as well as of the philosopher and the phallocrat. They are motivated by one desire: the desire for the same mind, the same meaning, the same standard, the same language. They promise enlightenment, emancipation, and empowerment. Yet in a postmodern culture, *ecriture féminine* joins with other forms of postmodern discourse in regarding "consensus [as] an outmoded and suspect value," as an instrument of totalization and totalitarianism (Lyotard, *Postmodern* 66). It breaks with the ideology of communication and seeks instead to explore the limits of language as a communicative system. (99)

Worsham believes that de Beaugrande's use of the term *genuinely non-aligned system of discourse* refers to a neutral discourse—"neutral with respect to position, bias, prejudice, ideology" (99). She contends that this seems to reflect an "Enlightenment dream of rationality," and she argues that "De Beaugrande quite shrewdly navigates the issue of difference, appropriating *ecriture féminine* in a way that makes difference a nonissue when for French feminists it is the only issue" (99).

Worsham's criticism of de Beaugrande is right on target. De Beaugrande does not bring French feminism to composition studies in ways that benefit both composition and French feminist theories—a difficult task in and of itself. In order for de Beaugrande to discuss French feminism in light of composition—or vice versa—French feminism necessarily loses out in his appropriation of it. De Beaugrande brings French feminism to composition not to further speculate about what French feminist theory says about discourse but in ways that serve to "use" it to promote composition's agenda. In doing so, French feminism becomes neutralized, loses its radical edge. Worsham sees this as the continued fate of *écriture féminine*—and of some feminisms, I believe—if composition continues its appropriation of feminist theory. She argues that "Composition theorists will effectively manipulate *ecriture féminine* to shore up the foundations of their field as a modernist discipline committed to the old dreams of the Enlightenment" (99).

WRITING (WITH) FEMINISMS

Like de Beaugrande's appropriation of French feminism, Junker's "Writing (with) Cixous" has also been targeted as bringing feminism to composition in ways that serve to neutralize the radical edge of French feminism. Junker claims that French feminism has had difficulty making its way into scholarly discussion about composition. She believes that while French feminist Hélène Cixous displays an enthusiasm for writing that surpasses that of many composition instructors, her alliance with "writing the body"—discourse that glorifies bodily fluids and an intimate awareness of the body—has frightened many in composition. Junker contends that "by opening ourselves to French (feminist) theories of writing, we teachers of composition, male and female, might actually engender new textual and pedagogical strategies within our field and beyond" (424).

Junker posits that while we might not be able to remove the discourses that have come to represent "woman" as they have, we might be able to disrupt them from "within" via our pedagogies. She claims that by not allowing language to become "a mere medium for transmitting from master to student" we might be able to "call attention to the mastery-knowledge-power connection by assiduously focusing on language itself, and, in the process, trace the represented otherness hiding within" (424). She understands the French feminists' critique of phallogocentrism to derive from a "Derridean strategy of reversing and deconstructing the binary trap in which 'woman' is caught in Western discourse" (425).

Drawing on Jacques Lacan, Junker posits that French feminists seek to distinguish between "biological females and a feminine linguistic position" (426). She says that what French feminists—particularly Cixous and Julia Kristeva—designate as *écriture féminine* "takes on qualities of the prelinguistic imaginary, the realm of bodily pleasures and drives untouched by castration and separation"—Lacan's position that woman must identify herself with lack (426). She posits that the agenda of French feminists "to write as 'woman' is thus to join a group of poetic revolutionists seeking to overturn established phallogocentric (sign) systems" (428). According to Junker, "what French feminists seek to liberate, then, is the tortured voice of the (wo)man imprisoned within 'phallogocentric systems of representation'" (428).

Turning to ways in which Cixous and other French feminists can be *used* by composition, Junker argues that while Cixous's "sexual/textual exuberance is foreign to the more pragmatic American composition specialists interested in writing (and) gender" her "tortured" feminine voice is not (428). For Junker, composition's approach to gender has traditionally been one of researching sexism in educational texts and a struggle against the generic pronoun *he*, yet she also notes that a few scholars have begun to address issues of feminist voice and an understanding of woman's "sense of non-ownership, and of disappointment at not being able to make herself heard" (429). Junker explores several texts that parallel French feminist thinking (texts by Edward M. White, Joan Bolker, Margaret B. Pigott, Pamela L. Annas, and Thomas J. Farrell) and argues that "French feminist theory thus parallels or even engenders (empirical) studies in rhetoric and composition in the United States" (431). However, she does point out that "offhand *l'ecriture féminine* and the (American) academy seem to be strange bedfellows indeed" (431).

In her attempt not to allow language to become "invisible," Junker suggests that perhaps sharing French feminist thought with composition "might help us to estrange our students from language while simultaneously restoring it to them" (432). She goes on to say that "by encouraging student writers to play with language, to stretch it, form it, caress it, we might give (back) to them the pleasure of the text" (432). She argues that classroom practice needs to stress the open-endedness of writing through revision and prewriting, and she contends that our teaching should emphasize "invention rather than conclusion" (432). She says that though it would be "trapped" within the confines of grades, exams, due dates, and other academic bureaucracy, this invention strategy would "take on the pleasurable, unconventional quality that Cixous associates with femininity and imaginary pulsions" (433). Drawing on Cixous's call for *écriture féminine*, Junker writes:

> What we can do as teachers of composition, then, is to allow for multiple kinds of writing, to invite our students into the *non-encore-là* and back again so as to encourage them to exist simultaneously in the realms of "reason and folly" (Conley, "Misstery" 75). Whether we consider the long-limbed athletes or the bright-eyed sorority pledges of freshman comp, our students are writing from a "feminine position," as from the margins they seek entry into the symbolic order of the university. By dislocating this order, we might enable student writers to (re)invent themselves and to inscribe *différance* in(side) academia. (434)

In essence, then, what Junker calls for—by way of Cixous and other French feminist theorists—is that student writers be encouraged to create discourses from their own voices rather than to merely reinscribe established phallogocentric discourses such as that of the academy.

Yet, like de Beaugrande, Junker's attempt to "dislocate" masculine discourse through composition pedagogy has received little scholarly attention, and the attention it does receive is critical. In her "Comment on 'Writing (with) Cixous,'" Debrah Raschke challenges Junker's "unqualified grouping" of Kristeva, Irigaray, and Cixous under the heading *French feminists*. Raschke points out that these three thinkers are very difficult to get a handle on individually, let alone together in a group, since their works have little in common with one another—a grouping that to Junker "seems less criminal than it does to Professor Raschke" ("Responds" 825). Raschke is even more eager to point out the problems presented in Junker's pedagogy. She contends that Junker, like Cixous, calls for students to write themselves; that is, she calls for *female* students to write themselves. Raschke argues that "In her concern with women's texts, Junker does not make it at all clear how this pedagogy would benefit the male students in the class" (823). While I think Junker intended her stereotyping phrase "whether we consider the long-limbed athletes or the bright-eyed sorority pledges of freshman comp" to imply all students, Raschke's criticism here leads to a more all-inclusive critique: that of the advocacy of self which Junker, by way of Bolker, calls for. Raschke is correct in her asking "how is this different from what many writing programs have been doing for the past several years? Remember the expressive theorists?" (823–24). Raschke commends Junker's call for effective writing strategies such as emphasizing invention and revision, but as she notes that these strategies may be seen as paralleling Cixous's, they have also been "operating in many of our composition classrooms since the emergence of the process approach to writing in the early seventies—long before any of us even thought of Cixous" (824).

Raschke agrees with Junker—and Cixous—"that in order for patriarchal systems to be changed, language usage as abstract, linear, and bounded, must also be changed," but her criticism is one of pragmatics (824). She asks if in all fairness we are to teach our students to write as Junker and Cixous advocate, "how many others in academe will look favorably on what Junker sees as positive feminine 'twirping, chattering, and clattering'?" (824). She explains that, even beyond academic recognition, to offer Junker's method of writing without also explaining its meaning or operation will only produce more "twirping" and "chattering" that will be designated a marginal discourse. Yet Junker, in her response to Raschke, is adamant that she would never simply offer her Cixousian method without the kinds of explanations that Raschke calls for; she pleads "did I ever say I would?" (826). In fact, Junker is quick to tie this separation between the operation, the implementation of her pedagogy, and the explanation of her theoretical grounding of that practice to the larger theory/anti-theory, theory/practice debates: "this dreaded divorce of theory and practice seems located in fears and/or desires altogether outside my article, though not, to be sure, outside the university" (826). In other words, Junker is conscious of Raschke's effort to find a split between Junker's practice, which is thoroughly outlined in her article, and her theory, which is also discussed in the same piece. Yet, as Junker points out, it seems that because she does not specifically describe how her theory *leads* to her practice, Raschke is not willing to make the "leap of faith" that brings Junker's theory into dialectic with her practice. Instead, Raschke seems to want Junker to lay out in black and white a method of Cixousian writing that also explains to students what it means and what its importance is. In other words, Raschke's criticism grows from a hard-line practice stance that challenges Junker based on a questioning of both her practice and the pragmatics of that practice—an issue with which Junker is less concerned.

Worsham is more concerned with the interaction between feminism and composition that Junker forwards. In a way similar to how she criticizes de Beaugrande's neutralizing of feminisms' radical edge, Worsham argues that both Junker and de Beaugrande are concerned with showing

> how *écriture féminine* works so that they can make it work in the interest of current writing theory and pedagogy. This strategy—"know how it works" in order "to make it work"— is part of the habitual gesture of scholarship in composition and is symptomatic of a dominant mode of political interpretation within the university. (95)

Worsham is critical of composition's desire to be able to "do theory." She argues that by attempting to understand how feminist theory works and then applying that theory to composition—that is, to *do* feminist theory—the convergence of the two stands to alter either or both the theory and composition. In the case of Junker's application of theory to composition pedagogy, Worsham contends that it is the (feminist) theory that loses. If the process of bringing *écriture féminine* to composition shifts from resistance to incorporation, she fears that neutralization is inevitable. If this is the case, she argues that

> then perhaps we can exercise prudence about the level at which *écriture féminine* is introduced into and incorporated by composition studies. We may conserve some of its energy by realizing that it has less to contribute to the industry of composition—to the development of a new theory of writing or to the design of textual and pedagogical strategies—than it does to an examination of how composition conducts itself as a theoretical enterprise. (98)

Worsham claims that Junker participates in a political interpretation of Cixous's work, an interpretation "for which the fundamental move is a denial of difference" (95). She argues that Junker's title— "Writing (with) Cixous"—identifies Junker's awareness that by attempting to "do" Cixous in composition, Cixous's "otherness" is rendered neutral and becomes part of the "sameness" of composition.

According to Worsham, Junker "knows her essay both rewrites—and therefore distorts—Cixous and attempts to (re)model theory and practice in terms of Cixous' brand of *écriture féminine*" (95). More simply put, for Worsham, bringing Cixous's theories to composition pedagogy serves to anesthetize the radical edges of these theories. Worsham claims that part of Junker's goal is to bring the strangeness of French feminist thought to the fore and to expose it in order to make it less foreign and more palatable—that is, more applicable—to compositionists.

Worsham further argues that Junker subsequently domesticates *écriture féminine* by creating a strategy by which it becomes a new source for textual and pedagogical models:

> If *écriture féminine* operates against models, concepts, ready-made modes of thought, then it is just as likely to operate against strategies, routines, plans, procedures—against techniques of any kind that, because they can be applied generally across different writing situations and by different writers, deny differences and annul singularities. (95)

Yet Junker is determined to bring Cixous to composition since doing so would possibly allow teachers of composition to "engender new textual and pedagogical strategies within our field and beyond" (424). Worsham labels this need to ground theory in accountable, recognizable practice a "pedagogical imperative" and the "will to pedagogy" (96). Here, Worsham positions her critique of Junker in the larger theory/anti-theory debate. A large part of the anti-theory stance in the academy—and in composition studies, in particular—grows from the sentiment that in order for theory to be of any use it must directly lead to useful pedagogy—that is, to practical application. Worsham understands that Junker needs to validate Cixousian theory through composition pedagogy in order for her, like other compositionists, to find it to be a *useful* theory. But, Worsham explains, French feminists "do not offer a theory or even a set of theories of writing—that is, if *theory* is understood as a systematic explanation of some phenomenon. They are not interested in formalizing *écriture féminine* to offer us what we think we need—a nugget of pure truth about writing" (96). That is, some theories (*écriture féminine*, for instance) are not conducive to creating pedagogies, yet they still improve our understanding of discourse.

However, since Junker *does* attempt to create pedagogies based on Cixousian theory, Worsham is compelled to criticize the ways in which Junker does so. She points out that beyond the neutralizing power of Junker's intersection of theory and practice and the politics of the pedagogical imperative, Junker's pedagogy, despite any posturing to the contrary, "does not successfully alter the deeply entrenched power relations between students and teacher in the university system. . . . Students know that power and knowledge flow from the top down: teachers still determine assignments and still have the power to give or deny students the right to their own voices" (96).

TEACHING CONFLICT

Like Junker, Jarratt also sees a need for feminism to engage composition pedagogy; yet, unlike Junker, Jarratt is critical of some ways in which feminist thinking comes to composition studies. For Jarratt, the question of the relationship between composition and feminism is a crucial one. She recognizes that both fields hold powerful potential for each other, but she questions their less-promising affinity: "a strong resistance to conflict" ("Conflict" 106). For Jarratt, some feminisms and some composition pedagogies resist the importance of conflict:

> Some feminists vigorously reject argument on the grounds that it is a kind of violence, an instrument specific to patriarchal discourse and unsuitable for women trying to reshape thought and experience by changing forms of language use. For some composition teachers, creating a supportive climate in the classroom and validating student experience leads them to avoid conflict. ("Conflict" 106)

This position, Jarratt argues, leaves students and teachers unprepared to "negotiate the oppressive discourses of racism, sexism, and classism surfacing in the composition classroom"—issues that, Jarratt claims, seem to be appearing even in classes not associated with those topics ("Conflict" 106).

Jarratt notes that some feminists have critiqued discourse—particularly, academic discourse—as a hierarchical, phallogocentric system. For example, she criticizes Sally Miller Gearhart for wanting to avoid the conflicts of language; Gearhart claims that "the difference between a persuasive metaphor and a violent artillery attack is obscure and certainly one of degree rather than kind" (197). For Gearhart, speaker-oriented communication is too violent; the act of one speaker trying to persuade another is an act of dominance. Gearhart calls for a more "peaceful" system of communication in which no one speaks to inform or persuade; instead, speakers express difference. Jarratt recognizes that it would be "too easy a game to point out the inconsistencies and contradictions in Gearharts' argument (for it is clearly that)" ("Conflict" 107). Yet she does point out that Gearhart's argument is seemingly reminiscent of models that compositionists of the sixties and seventies put forward: models that hoped to give students power in the classroom and to make teachers participants rather than overseers. Jarratt sees Gearhart's attitude about conflict as similar to that of many of composition's current student-oriented pedagogies. Many of these pedagogies were, at first, productive in that they encouraged students to write about what mattered to them and to challenge traditional institutional literary studies which had nothing to do with their lives. In other words, these pedagogies encouraged conflict.

Yet, frequently, when compositionists design pedagogies in which students work in groups, consensus seems to be a goal. For example, Peter Elbow's group-centered pedagogy works best with seven to twelve people who "have a lot in common," and he says participants should "never quarrel with someone else's reaction" (*Writing* 79, 95). Yet, we have come to recognize that in postmodern classrooms cultural issues—race, culture, gender, class, and so on— make it difficult for students to see their interactions with other students as equal. "Such inequities often make the attempt to create a harmonious and nurturing community of readers an illusionary fiction—a superficial suturing of real social divisions," as Jarratt points out ("Conflict" 110).

Jarratt argues that while expressivist pedagogies work to displace authority—a goal of many feminisms—expressivist composition pedagogies, Elbow's in particular, are problematic for feminism. Jarratt commends Elbow for *Writing without Teachers*, a book that she says is "truly a revolutionary text in its feminization of the male writing teacher" ("Conflict" 110). However, she is also critical of the role female students play in Elbow's pedagogy. She contends that asking a female student to openly accept every response in mixed-gendered classrooms encourages entrenched gender hierarchies: "advising a female student to 'swallow' without reply a conventional male reaction to a woman's experience has serious consequences" ("Conflict" 111).

Similarly, Jarratt argues that when a female teacher uses Elbow's nurturing classroom methods, she replicates the traditional female role: one in which women would be openly uncritical of male criticism.

Despite her criticisms of expressivist pedagogies, Jarratt recognizes that many feminists find them useful because they agree with Elbow and Donald Murray that composition teachers should be nurturing and nonconflictual. She cites the work that Elisabeth Däumer and Sandra Runzo have done to parallel writing instruction with the role of the mother. She also recognizes the ways in which Carol A. Stanger, by way of Carol Gilligan, has explored the possibilities of gender-related conflict in the classroom. More thoroughly, she examines two pedagogies which move "toward a more politically effacacious use of argument: one offered by feminist philosopher Joyce Treblicot in 'Dyke Methods or Principles for the Discovery/Creation of the Withstanding' and the other by a more rhetorical Elbow" ("Conflict" 114).

But for "pedagogies most fully engaged in issues of gender, race, and class—pedagogies in which conflict is central," Jarratt turns to the scholarship of Kathleen Weiler and the "radical black feminism of bell hooks" ("Conflict" 118). Jarratt contends that while the critical pedagogies of male scholars such as Henry Giroux and Paulo Freire tend to focus on issues of class, Weiler widens the reading of these scholars by bringing issues of gender to discussions of conflict. Jarratt also agrees with hooks's pedagogy which reacts against "an exclusive focus on personal experience as a simple inversion of the older pedagogy of domination against which compositionists reacted in the sixties and seventies" ("Conflict" 120).

Jarratt, by way of the theorists and practitioners she critiques, seeks to find "productive tension in the differences among feminists' positions" ("Conflict" 121). She argues that by recognizing the need to engage in conflict—that is, to "confront the different truths our students bring to our classes"—feminism and rhetoric and composition "become allies in contention with the forces of oppression troubling us all" ("Conflict" 121). Unlike Worsham, Jarratt sees productive interaction between feminist theories and composition pedagogies. Her applause for expressivist pedagogies that "feminize" composition instruction—particularly, male teachers—is a recognition that feminist philosophies (that is, feminist theories) *can* find their way into composition pedagogies. For Jarratt, theory and practice do interact in dialectical relationship. In *Rereading the Sophists: Classical Rhetoric Refigured*, she insists that we need both theory *and* practice in composition. In her reading of the sophists, she iden-

tifies sophistic "practice" as not being "confined to the classroom"—
an intellectual role that she believes should "be sought by
composition teachers today" (*Rereading* 95). In other words, for Jarratt, composition and feminist theory have much potential for
interaction. While she sees theory and practice as inseparable and
claims that compositionists should participate in both, Jarratt does
critique ways in which feminist theory is brought to composition; she
calls for further speculation, further theorizing, as to how the two
bodies of knowledge interact, react, and engage.

FEMINISM AND THE "IDENTITY" OF COMPOSITION

Feminist theories have other effects on the field
besides practical application. By bringing feminist theory to composition studies, Miller, for example, does not attempt to construct a
useful pedagogy; rather, she employs feminism(s) to identify the sim-
ilarity between the plights that feminism(s) face and those which
composition faces in the academy.

The integration of feminist theory into composition studies,
while creating tensions between feminism and composition, moves to
potentially gender-balance both composition research and pedagogy.
At the same time, feminisms have received much negative attention.
The theoretical integration of feminism into composition—as in
many other fields—is seen merely as the cries of a marginalized voice
demanding political action. Miller, in "The Feminization of Composition," offers a new reading of composition studies that "places both
the political action that we obviously need, and many new intellectual and practical movements toward gender balance in composition,
against a prevailing negative cultural identity that 'the feminization of
composition' implies" (39).

Miller forwards the phrase *call to identity* to "bring to mind a
group of related leftist political and feminist theories that explain
identity formation as a result of cultural context" (39). Within this
understanding of identity, Miller argues that for many feminist theorists, despite the qualities females may possess individually, their
cultural identity prescribes a call to "womanhood"—essentially a
"hood" to cloak difference and assure that identities (both male and
female) are defined by false imagined relations rather than actual
situations. Miller says, "This separation of genders first organized

cultures for their biological, economic, social survival"—a separation that ensures phallocentric regulation of status and power (40). She argues that this same power structure exists in composition studies. That is, within the academy, composition—its history and development—has been relegated to a marginal status from which compositionists call for political action, and their critics want their identity to be simply that of service to the community. Miller claims that composition plays the role of the "sad woman in the basement" and draws on Sue Holbrook's presentation of statistical analysis of composition to suggest that composition has been deemed "women's work" (*Textual* 121–41).

Miller's assessment of composition and her analogy to feminist struggle seem accurate. As I have mentioned before, composition is frequently relegated to a service in the academy. Compositionists are often viewed as serving only to mother students until they learn to "get it right" and can then leave the nest to engage in serious academic pursuits. The image of the ruler-totin' school marm comes to mind. Miller's tie between feminism and composition certainly helps us to better see how composition has been defined and how the field struggles to find identity, and, at the same time, her assessment pushes us to think more about ways in which composition has earned this position.

As several scholars have shown (for instance, see Golding and Mascaro or Dobrin "Writing"), when teachers impose blame for why their students "can't write," that blame is most often turned toward the teachers who taught the students first: graduate faculty blame undergraduate instructors; undergraduate instructors question whether first-year composition teachers are doing their jobs; first-year composition instructors argue that students should have learned to write in high school; and so on down the line. This refusal to take responsibility assumes a hands-off model for education: "why should I have to teach them what someone else was supposed to have taught them?" The inherent difficulty is that this attitude creates an image of composition as remedial work. This perception of writing instruction reminds me of the adage *actors wait tables and writers teach English*. These words have always echoed for me an unfair conventional wisdom that those of us who teach writing do so because we cannot get "real" jobs doing beneficial work or doing what we want to do. Teaching writing, it seems, has always held the position of summer work, of temporary labor, of what Miller calls "women's work" or what my (racist) grandfather might call "nigger's work."[6] While Miller is somewhat ironic in her label—and my grandfather deplorable in his—composition has certainly been viewed in a similar way.

Seeing composition instruction in this light helps bring into perspective many of the "events" that have shaped current thinking about composition. For instance, why is composition instruction in the academy staffed by a large population of underpaid, overworked part-time faculty? Without question, economics plays a large role in this, but, more to the point, composition courses—particularly required first-year courses—are not seen as academic courses; they are, in fact, perceived as a cattle drive: classes for the masses—that is, classes that everyone takes, everyone passes, and few actually leave better off than when they entered. Hence, the rationale evolves to let the "women" of the academy (the ruler-totin' school marms)— the compositionists—handle the menial labor. That is, why should the "real" scholars be wasted on a mere cattle drive? Perhaps my assessment here grows from anger. As I have mentioned before, rhetoric and composition has established itself as an intellectual field. However, in doing so, it has created an identity for itself and for how the academy sees it based on phallocentric power structures. Composition and the academy relegate composition instruction to marginalized status and to "women's work." Miller's effort to scrutinize composition studies by way of feminist thinking helps us understand the field in terms of how its identity has been shaped. Perhaps more than any other scholar, Miller has—by way of feminist thinking—helped reexamine not only how composition is taught but also how the field of rhetoric and composition has evolved in similar ways to feminist thinking, in ways that encourage interaction between composition and feminism.

FEMINIST (ACADEMIC) DISCOURSE

Like other theories that have become influential in composition's development, feminist theory has been imported to serve pedagogical needs, has been criticized because it cannot serve those needs without altering original theoretical agendas of feminism, and has helped us (re)envision the field's identity. For Flynn and Junker, validation of these theories comes through their applicability to pedagogy, while for Worsham such translations to application serve to neutralize the very purpose of some feminist theories. In both instances of exploration of how feminist theory interacts with composition pedagogy, issues about phallogocentric (academic) discourse become predominant.

Few feminist theorists or practitioners would not argue that one of the major goals of feminist theory's interaction with composition is an attempt to recognize the ways in which discourse—particularly, academic discourse—and gender engage each other. Frequently, this interaction is put forward as a need for feminist discourse to disrupt traditional phallogocentric academic discourse. However, despite the revolutionary goals of feminist discourse(s), feminist scholars are generally wary to admit that such radical intervention is contradictory. By assuming that feminist discourse can serve to discredit, disrupt, or disempower academic discourse, those who put forward these theories fail to recognize that feminist discourse is itself academic discourse.[7] The feminist discourse that scholars discuss in relation to composition studies is promoted only within the academy; it is a form of academic discourse. We do not read or hear similar discussion outside the academy, in popular media, or in everyday conversations. Simply put, we cannot discuss feminist theory and its implications for improving writing instruction, for advancing our understanding of discourse, for helping us to better locate composition's identity without relying on a variation of the very academic discourse (some) feminist theory seeks to disrupt. Perhaps this disruption and introduction of new academic discourse is beneficial, but it is still a system of academic discourse. How can we discuss feminist discourse, academic discourse, without using the very discourses and theories that are already in place to critique them?

Certainly, feminist theory has the potential both to improve composition pedagogies and to open our eyes to new ways to see the operation of discourse—traditional or radically revolutionary discourse. While I agree with Worsham that many of these new radical theories stand to lose their edge as they are brought to composition, without engaging feminist theory and composition, neither body of knowledge stands to gain from the other. Perhaps it is the compromise between altering composition as we now know it and whittling down feminist theories that stands to create a more "feminine" understanding of written discourse, and perhaps of how we teach. It seems that as scholars bring composition and feminisms together there is a need to suggest new, more pedagogically and theoretically satisfactory vehicles through which the two can inter(re)act. As we create these new vehicles, we have two options: build upon the foundations of discredited structures, or just build new ones in unoccupied margins. Yet in doing so, we must not avoid conflict. Conflict between composition and feminism stands to perpetuate thought and discussion, and conflict within the classroom stands to better students' understanding of language and serves to help push at the very borders and confines of that language. I have quoted Joy Ritchie in one of my epigraphs as arguing that the split between feminist theory and pedagogy is artificial; yet, in composition scholarship, there is a definite distinction as some feminist theories find difficulty in moving toward pedagogy. Perhaps by placing feminist theory and scholarship into a transformative dialectic, each will enhance the other.

5

IDEOLOGY, LITERACY, AND RADICAL PEDAGOGY IN COMPOSITION STUDIES

> "I think we are talking about literacy because we are having a collective identity crisis about being English teachers, and, in particular, we are very unclear as to what good we are doing for the larger society with our efforts."
>
> — *Patricia Bizzell, "Professing Literacy: A Review Essay"*

> "A rhetoric can never be innocent, can never be a disinterested arbiter of the ideological claims of others because it is always already serving certain ideological claims."
>
> — *James Berlin, "Rhetoric and Ideology in the Writing Class"*

A quick glance at recent scholarship in composition and in other academic areas reveals a trend to emphasize literacy. For instance, at the 1994 Conference on College Composition and Communication Convention, in excess of a hundred sessions were listed as pertaining to the "Politics of Literacy" or "Contexts for Writing and Literacy." The theoretical issue of literacy is complex and has great impact on how we view composition and rhetoric as a field of study and how we teach writing. Because we have begun to recognize that literacy involves more than the acquisition of certain "skills," compositionists have also begun to examine ways in which social ideologies influence not only how we teach writing and how students learn writing but also how we conceive of the very nature of what *literacy* is. What makes the interaction between (what I will call) "literacy theory" and composition so interesting is that for the first time in intellectual history we have come to recognize the impact that ideology has on knowledge making; we understand that knowledge is indeed a social construction. This new understanding of knowledge inherently affects our view of written discourse. We have begun to understand that the very societal effects on knowledge making must necessarily also affect discourse in all its forms.

A language of crisis permeates discussions of literacy. Our perception—that is, the academy's and the general public's—has grown from a belief that students are simply not as literate as they should be. In composition, we have answered this call of crisis and begun to explore various avenues that might lead to a better understanding of exactly what it means to be "literate." From conversations of basic writing pedagogy to the recent explosion of scholarship on race, gender, class, and cultural studies, compositionists have pushed the field in a direction that identifies written discourse and the teaching of writing as more than a simple set of closed-capacity skills that one must "acquire" in order to be literate. Literacy theory has come to composition in ways that perhaps have altered our thinking about the field as no other recent theory has.

IDEOLOGY

Ideology is perhaps the most central issue to current discussions of literacy, literacy theory, and radical pedagogy. In many ways, composition studies has recently become devoted to ideology studies as we come to recognize that ideology is entwined in/with discourse. So completely, in fact, have we recognized the close link between discourse and ideology that discerning between the two becomes more of a strategic maneuver than an actual distinction. Ideology is the site of discourse, and understanding the relationship between ideology, culture, literacy, and discourse has come to the fore in current composition theory. This relationship, however, is not easily defined, as *ideology* often stands as a significant theoretical problem.[1]

In composition—as in other fields that engage ideology theory—the models that Louis Althusser presents in "Ideology and Ideological State Apparatuses" are frequently seen as the primary definition of *ideology*. However, as compositionists began to adopt these models in the 1970s, many who were discussing ideology began to argue that these models are deterministic and mechanical. Cultural critic Stuart Hall, for instance, argues that

> discourse . . . had the effect of sustaining certain "closures,"
> of establishing certain systems of equivalence between what
> could be assumed about the world and what could be said to

be true. "True" means credible, or at least capable of winning credibility as a statement of fact. New problematic or troubling events, which breached the taken-for-granted expectancies about how the world should be, could then be "explained" by extending to them the forms of explanation which have served "for all practical purposes," in other cases. In this sense, Althusser was subsequently to argue that ideology, as opposed to science, moved constantly within a closed circle, producing, not knowledge, but a recognition of things we already knew. It did so because it took as an already established fact exactly the premises which ought to have been put in question. (75)

Unlike many compositionists, Hall warns against collapsing ideology and language into a singular event. He argues that they are not the same thing and that ideology is articulated through language. At the same time, he argues that as we come to understand ideology to influence knowledge making and meaning, meaning must not be reduced to an issue of class struggle:

Though discourse could become an arena of social struggle, and all discourse entailed certain definite premises about the world, this was not the same thing as ascribing ideologies to classes in a fixed, necessary or determinate way. Ideological terms and elements do not necessarily belong in this definite way to classes; and they do not necessarily and inevitably flow from class positions. (80)

Of course, composition theorists have recently come to view ideology, class, and language as interacting with one another. Since these early encounters with Althusserian ideology, compositionists have come to highlight both the ideological effects of discourse and the effects of discourse on ideology.

As Althusser's ideology became more and more scrutinized, his theory limited the explanation of the relationship between culture, ideological structure, and the individual subject; as David Morley explains, "it is not simply Althusser who is at issue here; much of the psychoanalytic work on the theory of ideology generates an equally passive notion of subjectivity, in which the subject is precisely 'spoken' by the discourses which constitute the person" (43). In need of more applicable definitions and understandings of ideology and wishing to spurn the classical marxist notion of ideology, compositionists began to turn toward the works of Michel Foucault and of Antonio Gramsci for different views of the operations of ideology. Foucault's discussions of power and ideology pushed compositionists to understanding the controlling value of ideology (see Chapter Two), and Gramsci's theory of hegemony brought the issues of culture and contestation to the fore. While prefiguring Althusser's concentration on the role of ideology and the state, Gramsci began to introduce an intersection of culture and ideology that departed from traditional marxist notions. He argues that the cultural and ideological relationship between ruling and oppressed classes is less an issue of domination than it is of a push toward hegemony—the idea that control is not achieved through manipulation of the masses but that controlling classes must engage in negotiations with those who oppose their views, must legitimately accommodate opposing views, and that hegemony succeeds not by eliminating the opposition but by dissolving it through the *articulation* of assimilation:

> Hegemony implied that the dominance of certain formations was secured, not by ideological compulsion, but by cultural leadership. It circumscribed all those processes by means of which dominant class alliance or ruling bloc, which has effectively secured mastery over the primary economic processes in society, extends and expands its mastery over society in such a way that it can transform and re-fashion its ways of life, its *mores* and conceptualization, its very form and level of culture and civilization in a direction, which while not directly paying immediate profits to the narrow interests of any particular class, favors the development and expansion of the dominant social and productive system of life as a whole. The critical point about this concept of "leadership"—which was Gramsci's most distinguished contribution—is that hegemony is understood as accomplished, not without the due measures of legal and legitimate compulsion, but principally by means of winning the active consent of those classes and groups who were subordinated within it. (Hall 85)

While Gramsci, Althusser, Foucault, and others who promote understandings of ideology certainly pushed our thinking about ideology to what it has become, there has also been a recent turn to dispel some of the more established understandings about ideology.

Michel de Certeau, for instance, argues for the reaction of marginalized groups against institutional and hegemonic control. Similarly—and perhaps more widely appropriated in composition—Mikhail Bakhtin's theory of the "carnivalesque" is frequently (and perhaps inappropriately) interpreted as a means of resistance by way of illicit and offensive pleasure. Likewise, Roland Barthes's *Jouissance* extends pleasure beyond ideology because of its natural rather than cultural origins.

Even as these kinds of resistance to ideological control began to surface, postmodern thinking in composition also began to reconsider particularly the role of ideology. We have come to recognize the heterogenous nature of everyday activity; we recognize that writing—discourse in general—contains more complexities than the simple all-encompassing labels of *ideology* explain. We use metaphors of ideology and look for ways to step beyond or refute those metaphors. We have reconsidered how ideology, culture, race, gender, class, and discourse all interact and react, particularly in terms of literacy and education.

More recently, discussions about the role of ideology have become more prevalent, and such discussions problematize how we view learning and teaching. We have come to recognize that ideologies are already embedded in everything we do and are reinscribed through discourse, through teaching. Yet in the many discussions about literacy and ideology, defining *ideology* seems as elusive as the concept itself, or as James Berlin puts it, "Ideology is a term of great instability" (478). Many scholars have offered good definitions, but few can come to consensus as to what exactly *ideology* is.

Because the concept of ideology is such a slippery one to grasp and because defining *ideology* is problematic, scholars frequently turn to metaphors to promote a particular understanding of the concept or term. Anne Haas-Dyson, for instance, explains one version of a popular metaphor that relates ideology to being like a fish in water:

> There is an old saying about a fish—that it would be the last to discover water because, outside that water, a fish has no existence, no self; the water provides the resources for its everyday life and, also, the constraints of that life. Moreover, its sense of self (if such sense were possible), of being a fish of a particular size, speed, color, or other quality, would depend upon its relationship to other fish in its sea and on the historical, cultural, and political milieu that marked certain qualities as significant. (15–16)

Some scholars further this metaphor and describe *ideology* as being particularly like fish in a fishbowl in that we must exist in its water, yet, like an agitated fish, by occasionally jumping out, disturbing the surface, and glancing back at the ripples, we can catch quick glimpses of ideology—though we must necessarily fall back into it.

Of course, this metaphor is flawed. By suggesting that one can even temporarily leap from the grasp of ideology suggests that one can obtain an objective view not only of how ideology operates but also of the natural order of the world. Certainly, we have come to recognize that not even for brief moments can we escape the ideologies that shape our thinking, our perceptions, our knowledge. Perhaps the most vivid refutation of this metaphor comes indirectly from Gary Larson's March 30, 1988, "Far Side." In this cartoon, several goldfish are seen standing outside of their fishbowl staring back into it at their fish house, which is engulfed in flames; apparently, they have narrowly escaped. The caption—the voice of one of the now homeless fish—reads, "Well, thank God we all made it out in time. . . . 'Course, now we're equally screwed." Although Larson relies on the bizarre irony for a well-deserved laugh, the cartoon mirrors this metaphor of ideology in that escaping the flames that are located in ideology leaves us floundering. Larson again inadvertently refutes the fishbowl metaphor in his March 23, 1992, cartoon, in which two fish in a fishbowl are seen talking to each other: "I guess he made it . . . it's been more than a week since he went over the wall." Lying on the floor just under the table where the fishbowl sits is the skeletal remains of what is apparently the one fish who tried to flee the confines of the bowl. Existence beyond the fishbowl is not possible.

A more applicable metaphor came to the fore during a discussion following a panel regarding ideology and dialogism at the 1993 CCCC convention in San Diego.[2] Following the comments of an angered audience member who insisted that she did not teach from an ideological standpoint but rather was able to teach her students about writing objectively, panel members attempted to explain what they meant by the term *ideology*. In doing so, they forwarded the metaphor that ideology operated much like a flexible tunnel that surrounds us. Frequently, we may suffer from tunnel vision and not recognize that the tunnel actually surrounds us or that we exist in that tunnel, although it actually controls the direction in which we move and how and what we see. However, by applying pressure to that tunnel at certain points, we are occasionally able to bend the tunnel, create curves in its direction, and in doing so, we are able to catch occasional glimpses of its sides as it refracts and arches. In other words, we are not able to escape it, but we can occasionally affect its direction and occasionally gain an impression of the ways it controls our lives, our knowledge.

Current thinking about ideology in these terms has come to recognize, then, that knowledge is not something that educators can objectively transmit to students, nor can students simply ingest information in some pure form. Rather, we have come to recognize that ideology *does* affect both learning and teaching and that traditional "banking" methods of education deny students agency in *what* and *how* they learn. Hence, discussions regarding what it means to be literate have shifted drastically in recent years under this relatively new understanding of ideology, and because of this, scholarly conversations about literacy and ideology have had a good deal of impact on how we think about pedagogy. It seems that when discussing literacy theory—particularly, when in relation to composition—the pedagogical imperative or the connections between theory and practice are more direct.

Through our conversations about ideology, culture, literacy, and, in turn, radical pedagogy, we have begun to recognize that we have the chance to expose our students to more than simple investment learning, wherein educators deposit "knowledge" in students or students acquire the "true" knowledge that educators offer them. Rather, we have begun to acknowledge that the ideological assumptions of instructors as well as of students impact how students learn and how and what instructors teach. In other words, current understandings of literacy—and radical pedagogies that promote literacy—begin a movement toward empowerment, toward the return of agency.

Contemporary thinking about pedagogy—particularly, the vastly important impact that Paulo Freire's radical pedagogy has had on our thinking about teaching—recognizes that teaching has traditionally been seen as a banking method of education. That is, for many decades now we have played a type of "I know/you don't know" game with our students. We have robbed students of their agency by denying them the opportunity to make critical and evaluative decisions and judgments about how and what they learn. By giving students the opportunity to understand the ideological and epistemological standpoint of their instructor, students are then positioned to judge and decide how and what they learn—what they choose to value in what their instructors present.

Traditionally, our own ideological situatedness was kept from students. Because we each come to the classroom from our own situated position with our own epistemological, pedagogical, and theoretical assumptions, how we teach writing is greatly affected by our situatedness. In the past, when we played this game with our students, we assumed that these "ideologies" didn't matter; we assumed, under the old paradigm, that we could teach (writing) objectively. However, within the postmodern paradigm, we recognize that this is not possible. We frequently hear the radical liberatory agenda of returning agency to students, of encouraging them to be critically conscious of their world. It is specifically this perception that moves toward returning to students the agency of which traditional Enlightenment-rationality's understanding of education has robbed them.

Scholars in composition such as David Bartholomae, Patricia Bizzell, John Clifford, John Schilb, and Victor Vitanza, and scholars as diverse as Stephen Toulmin, Stanley Fish, Richard Rorty, Jean François Lyotard, and Donna Haraway, who come from various other disciplines, have begun to recognize that the ideological position from which an individual operates has great impact on—in fact, controls—how that individual manipulates, learns, and passes on knowledge. That is to say, by assuming that we can teach from an ideology-free zone, we deny our students—and ourselves—an opportunity to engage not only the material at hand but the ideologies from which that understanding of that material grows. For instance, to be able to say to our students, "I operate from a social constructionist understanding of discourse," or "I believe in the expressivist vision of writing" allows students to see that when we convey information about writing we do not convey an objective "truth" about writing but rather an understanding of writing from a standpoint that arises from a particular set of ideological assumptions. For the most part, educators have denied the important role that ideology plays both in how we teach and in how students learn.

FALSE ALARM(?)

As with *ideology*, defining *literacy* is a difficult task, and a comprehensive definition of the term is problematic. Because literacies vary, what literacy is supposed to accomplish in various contexts may also differ. Yet with all of the discussion about ideology, literacy, how we teach literacy, how we achieve literacy, and so on, many, including Maureen M. Hourigan, suggest that "a comprehensive definition of literacy is precisely what is needed in the current discourse where 'literacy' has become a catchall term of many meanings" (xiv).

Richard Ohmann points out that definitions of literacy traditionally distinguished between those who could read and those who could not (216). Both Ohmann and Hourigan identify that over the past one hundred years or so our understanding of literacy has greatly evolved from this early perception, and both offer thorough reviews of the historical development of defining literacy—Hourigan in terms of crisis and Ohmann in terms of technology and monopoly capital. Yet as these scholars bring the issue of literacy to current debate, both agree that a social definition of literacy seems more appropriate to current conversations. Hourigan turns to Ohmann's definition to advance her own:

> It is not helpful to think of literacy as an invariant, individual skill, or as a skill whose numerically measurable distribution across society (as in *literacy rate*) will tell us much of scholarly interest or human relevance. Literacy is an activity of social groups, and a necessary feature of some kinds of social organization. Like every other human activity or product, it embeds social relations within it. And these relations always include *conflict* as well as cooperation. Like language itself, literacy is an exchange between classes, races, the sexes, and so on. (qtd. in Hourigan xiv).

Ohmann goes on to argue that "technique is less important than context and purpose in the teaching of literacy, and the *effects* of literacy cannot be isolated from the social relations and processes within which people become literate" (228). Similarly, Hourigan argues for a social definition of literacy, particularly in terms of what has become known as "critical literacy": that literacy which does not accept knowledge at face value but instead, as Hourigan cites Linda Flower, "questions sources, looks for assumptions, and reads intentions, not just facts" (5).

In terms of this social definition and the historical path by which this definition has evolved, Hourigan and Ohmann—along with numerous others who address literacy—have come to recognize that conversations about literacy have generally been forwarded in terms of *crisis*. Both Ohmann and Hourigan turn to Merrill Sheils's renowned 1975 *Newsweek* article, "Why Johnny Can't Write," as the epitome of how mass culture views the "literacy crisis." While Ohmann and Hourigan both offer succinct explanations as to how this culmination of crisis politics evolved historically, I am more concerned with how compositionists address this "crisis" in terms of pedagogy.

Perhaps one of the most influential scholars of literacy for composition has been Henry Giroux, who argues that conversations about literacy and crisis frequently refer to marginalized students. Giroux argues that literacy theories and the pedagogical approaches that grow from them seek to enfranchise marginalized—"illiterate"—groups into the mainstream by pointing out to them how social contexts affect their lives. In other words, we have traditionally viewed literacy as "the ability to read and write," and the educational institution—the academy—has viewed those who cannot do so as being in need of having literacy, and thereby agency, bestowed upon them. Traditionally, the politics of literacy has been such that in order for an individual to be "literate," that individual must meet academic standards—that is, must be able to read and write. Hence, "Why Johnny Can't Write" epitomizes a political view that literacy is institutionally defined by the academy. At the same time, because literacy rates under this definition were presumed to be low (Hourigan points out that because of the extreme difficulty in defining *literacy*, it is actually impossible to measure "literacy rates"), there was a "crisis" in that too many individuals did not meet institutional standards.

Of course, under this limited understanding of literacy, the academy—as well as institutional forces outside of the academy—deemed it necessary to bring everyone up to standard and make everyone "literate." Giroux argues that a good deal of the literatization that occurs takes place in remedial classes—classes particularly developed for those who have not yet achieved the status of being literate. He posits that literacy, then, is seen not as a social issue but instead in terms of a deficit theory of learning. That is to say, under these tags, literacy is not an activity of social groups but an issue of economics: an "I have/you don't have" game we play with students wherein we charitably give to the less fortunate and deposit knowledge into their knowledge accounts. Giroux argues that such systems and understandings of literacy deny individuals agency and the opportunity to lead active, participatory lives. Hence, the practical approaches that Giroux, compositionists interested in radical pedagogies, the academy, and those outside of the academy promote do not converge at any point to offer a solution—or even an explanation—for the "crisis" so many argue is at hand.

Discussions of literacy, whether they arise out of the radical left, the liberal left, the right, or the radical right, all participate in the same discourse, one whose systemic well-being is dependent upon the participation of all of these parties. Attempts to reframe or even expand this discourse are often seen as fundamental restructurings when they are in fact only alterations in the system. Consequently, new theories of literacy do not necessarily offer ground-breaking solutions to the "crisis," since the crisis itself is an integral part of the discursive system. That is, as Hourigan and Ohmann both clearly show, the "crisis" of literacy is not new. It has not emerged as an immediate concern; rather, we have been under the onslaught of this crisis since we began institutionalizing education. Those of us who are concerned with issues of literacy must recognize that, ultimately, literacy debates are defined by strategic maneuvers more so than moral or ethical positions, as Hourigan's historical assessment suggests. In their writings about literacy, scholars frequently mistakenly associate the systemic nature of discourse with the moral and ethical effects they hope to achieve. Frequently in our discussions about literacy we mistakenly attempt to devise pedagogies that we hope to serve as local panaceas for an ethical crisis of literacy that we have constructed from traditional theories of literacy. In other words, by bringing radical pedagogical theories directly to the classroom to help solve the problems that our theories of literacy dictate exist, we assume that it is our duty as educators to use these theories to create pedagogies to cure the problems of literacy we assume exist. Just as Bizzell suggests that part of our reason for discussing literacy stems from our identity crisis, our inability to figure out what we do for the common good, I believe that our overt eagerness comes from a desire to see liberatory learning as an antidote for a crisis that may not necessarily exist—or at least not in the terms by which we have defined it.

Patricia Harkin and John Schilb suggest that we have come to use the term *literacy crisis* as a way of codifying a particular group of individuals by offering a solitary "diagnosis" for what is viewed as an ailment. Harkin and Schilb draw a useful connection between this medical analogy for the crisis politics of literacy and Foucault's analyses of "institutions such as prisons, mental hospitals, and the military" all of which categorize and control individuals under labels "other than normal and in need of remediation" (2). Turning to Foucault's *Madness and Civilization*, Harkin and Schilb compare incarceration in the Hôpital Général because of afflictions that "contemporary science might, in its own institutional language, name . . . poverty, homelessness, and disease" to the literacy crisis (2). Despite the various "afflictions," the Hôpital Général simply isolated these individuals from the outside world, since they "fell outside the institutionalized notion of 'normal'" not for particulars (2). Harkin and

Schilb see this institutionalized imprisonment as analogous to the "literacy crisis"—particularly, that of the seventies—that identified as not being literate all students such as those

> who used minority dialects, nonnative speakers of English, white middle-class college students whose SAT scores were lower than those of their parents, people who lacked experience with the conventions of academic discourse, unemployed adults who could not read the instructions for filling out their welfare applications, and soldiers who failed to comprehend the instructions for making and deploying nuclear weapons. (3)

In other words, strategically, the term *literacy crisis* came to function as an "umbrella term to cover and isolate those persons who, for what ever reason, did not have 'normal' standards for discourse" (3). Just as the crisis itself can be seen as a strategy for control, so too can we view how we argue about literacy as a self-perpetuating strategy. As Harkin and Schilb say, quoting Paul Noack, "if we define crisis as a permanent status, . . . then crisis management itself will become permanent" (72). Perhaps it already has.

Harkin and Schilb argue that crisis management, then, is a political strategy that allows a social issue to be more easily controlled. They contend that "by creating new institutions, books, journals, Ph.D. programs, and conferences to deal with smaller and narrower aspects of 'literacy,'" the academy is practicing a management politics just as the literacy crisis has practiced a strategic literacy politics (3). Hence, the self-perpetuating nature of this understanding of literacy, literacy crisis, literacy management, and literacy debate not only calls for further conversation, further debate, further theorizing about these issues but also demands that how we have both traditionally and currently altered our views of literacy be explored if we are to find relevant ways of either continuing this discussion or moving beyond it.

LITERACY DEBATES

I remember, years ago, one of my professors asking, "What is literacy?" on the first day of a graduate composition class titled "Literacy and Culture" and then being asked to offer a short definition of *literacy*. As we were asked to share our definitions, there was a surprising consistency in all of the students' responses, a kind of consensus. What it amounted to was that we all understood literacy to imply "knowing the same things that everyone else knows." That is, consensus in knowledge constitutes literacy: if I know what other people know, I can exchange knowledge with them. However, current thinking about literacy and the recent explosion of scholarship to address literacy has sought to expand the definition beyond this oversimplified version.

A quick glance at recent scholarship in composition reveals that there must be substantially more to literacy than mere consensus. Important scholars in composition such as Bizzell, Lil Brannon, C. H. Knoblauch, Andrea Lunsford, Helene Moglen, and James Slevin have turned their attention to bringing literacy theory to composition, both in practical applicable ways and in ways that promote reexamination of both literacy and of composition as an area of study. In fact, more frequently than not, when scholars engage literacy—both in composition and outside—they do so with the intent to "redefine," "rewrite," or "reexamine" literacy.

Bizzell, one of composition's most outspoken and prolific scholars in addressing literacy, begins her essay "Professing Literacy: A Review Essay" by acknowledging that it is perhaps necessary to "redefine 'literacy' from within English studies in such a way as to make it more complex and problematic" (315). She argues that the simple definitions of "being able to read and write" that have been associated with literacy are no longer adequate as concepts of literacy diverge. Bizzell points out that even under the heading *literacy*, essays gathered in collections such as *The Right to Literacy* do not conform to a unified notion of literacy as the title might suggest. But Bizzell is less concerned with inscribing a formal definition; rather, she is concerned with why academics are "so interested in talking about literacy" and how the concept is being used, "however flexible its parameters" (316).

In her "Arguing about Literacy," Bizzell brings the conflict between literacy and academic discourse to the fore. According to her,

> arguments about literacy typically take the same form. One kind of literacy holds a commanding position, that which comprises the ways of using language valued by the academy and the upper social classes with which it is associated. The dominance of this academic literacy is challenged by people who have made their way into the schools but whose native tongues are at a relatively greater remove from the

academic dialect, whose preferred modes of developing ideas
conflict with the linear logic and impersonal posture of academic debate, and whose cultural treasures are not included
in the academic canon. (238)

So, for Bizzell, literacy—and by implication literacy debates—is
called into question most frequently by "social groups at some
remove from the upper classes—that is, from the lower classes,
foreign born, nonwhite, and/or female" (238). Bizzell's social spin
on literacy grows from her understanding that in the social sciences "research in literacy assumes that some decisive change
takes place when individuals and societies acquire literacy" (239).
Yet she also notes that in social science examinations of literacy
attention is paid to effects both on the individual and on society.
That is, in the social sciences, research in literacy moves toward a
view of multiple literacies.

However, literacy has come to composition in more crucial ways
through humanists who identify changes in discourse and by way of
those changes how culture changes.[3] Unlike scholarship in the social
sciences, work in the humanities on literacy—"The Great Cognitive
Divide"—argues that oral culture "is characterized in its verbal style
and in its thinking by parataxis, the simple juxtaposition of ideas; by
concrete imagery that appeals to the senses and the emotions; by
ritualized references to authority in the form of proverb, epithets,
incantations, and other formulae, and by antagonistic posture in
disposition" (Bizzell 240). Following this understanding of oral literacy, Bizzell posits that humanists "assert that the change from
oral thinking to literate thinking can be achieved only through acquisition of alphabetic literacy, and that it is always achieved when
alphabetic literacy has been acquired" (241). This suggests that the
debate surrounding the understanding of "what literacy *is*" may be
approached from various angles, none of which seems to disprove
the others.

And yet Bizzell is conscious of literacy and ideology. She repeatedly acknowledges the "unfair" agenda academic institutions
impose by dictating academic discourse as the only acceptable discourse. She identifies the exclusionary position academics take and
the "shirking of our professional responsibility simply to expel from
the academy those students who do not share our discourse"
("Beyond" 256). And, at the same time, she does not deny the crucial role that ideology and ethics play in the classroom. She is
critically aware that

everything I do in the classroom is informed by one or another element in my world view, thus potentially conflicting at every turn with other elements in the students' diverse world views and, because of my institutional position at the head of the class, potentially undercutting their values. ("Afterword" 284)

Despite this recognition, she makes no attempt to conceal the fact that her "world view" also brings a particular set of moral values to the classroom, and she readily admits that her classroom work is "deeply imbued with [her] moral values" ("Afterword" 284). In her introduction to *Academic Discourse and Critical Consciousness*, Bizzell begins to trace the ways in which her thinking about composition— both pedagogy and theory—evolved through her career. Through her early desires to use the composition classroom to promote social equality and her introduction to Freirean liberatory learning until her more recent concerns regarding anti-foundational positions, Bizzell has forwarded a social, cultural understanding of literacy that emphasizes cultural context.

CULTURAL LITERACY

Bizzell acknowledges that while many competing theories of literacy have come to the fore in literacy debates the concept of cultural literacy has emerged as a response to these debates. Cultural literacy suggests that "all literacy is in fact cultural literacy—that is, that no symbol system in and of itself induces cognitive changes. A cultural context is necessary to invest the features of the system with meaning, to give them the significance that then induces changes in thinking" ("Arguing" 242). In other words, Bizzell argues that the concept of cultural literacy evolves from an understanding that despite the sign systems on which a particular literacy depends that literacy would not exist outside of its cultural context.

Perhaps one of the most frequently criticized discussions of cultural literacy has been that of E. D. Hirsch in *The Philosophy of Composition, Cultural Literacy: What Every American Needs to Know* and in two articles titled "Cultural Literacy." In these discussions, Hirsch argues that "to be culturally literate is to possess the basic information needed to thrive in the modern world" (*What* xxiii). But part of Hirsch's aim is to promote "standard English" as the cultural norm and to provide a particular conception of what specifically that information is. Hirsch attempts to define what literacy *is*—particularly academic literacy—in what Bizzell calls a "definition that transcends social contexts and the local ideological agendas to which they give rise" ("Arguing" 243). In other words, Hirsch attempts to lay down a foundational understanding of what "true" literacy is and to identify a body of knowledge that all Americans should know in order to be able to participate in national public forums, and in doing so he neglects the recognition of local context.

Hirsch argues that all students should master "standard English," since it is the most "communicatively efficient" form of the language. But Hirsch is also definite in what he means by standard English and even carries his argument to the point of imposing a list of what information a "culturally literate" American would need to know. But this idea—the act of imposing concepts—is criticized for its social and political bias. Hirsch assumes that reading and writing are not independent of context, that it is necessary to also teach a standard context. Bizzell criticizes Hirsch for attempting to

> justify teaching a privileged dialect to everyone so that everyone can participate in the national life; but in order to make this case he has to ignore the fact that there are privileged people for whom the grapholect is much closer to a native tongue than it is for others, and who hence will have an advantage in mastering this condition for political participation. ("Introduction" 16)

That is to say, Bizzell argues against Hirsch's position since social class difference problematizes access to Hirsch's standardized dialect. But for Hirsch the problem of exclusion that grows from social class difference can be solved through education.

Bizzell notes in "Beyond Anti-Foundationalism to Rhetorical Authority: Problems Defining 'Cultural Literacy'" that Hirsch reaches this end by way of assumptions similar to those of many compositionists. For instance, she argues that Hirsch identifies "sharing a discourse" as "not only sharing a tongue but also sharing a mass of contextual knowledge that renders the tongue significant" (257). Like compositionists who argue that many students are not illiterate but just lack the cultural knowledge of academic discourse, Hirsch sees a need to share a common contextual conception of information in order to be able to share in a cultural literacy.

Of course, even from his earliest discussions of cultural literacy, Hirsch received a good deal of criticism from sources other than

Bizzell (see John Warnock's "Cultural Literacy: A Worm in the Bud?" for instance). In fact, MLA's *Profession 88* presented several critiques of Hirsch's cultural literacy: Paul B. Armstrong criticizes Hirsch's cultural literacy as a deceptive quick fix and argues against his singular definition of both "culture" and "literacy" as overly monistic; Andrew Sledd and James Sledd argue that Hirsch misrepresents the work of others in order to achieve his goals; Moglen argues that Hirsch's cultural literacy is no more than a farce; and in the exchange that concludes the issue, Hirsch, Sledd and Sledd, Armstrong, and Moglen continue to argue the validity of cultural literacy. While the *Profession 88* critiques represent a small fraction of the criticism that Hirsch has received for his work, Bizzell argues that much of the backlash against Hirsch—particularly, that in *Profession 88*—grows from a politically correct position rather than a position that legitimately engages Hirsch's work[4] (Dobrin and Taylor 63). That is, much of the criticism of Hirsch may deny the opportunity to look at Hirsch's theories in terms of what they offer as explanation of how we understand knowledge making and sharing.

Certainly, when Hirsch suggests that for an individual to obtain *literacy* or *to be literate* that individual must be familiar with a particular body of knowledge, he is correct in assuming that *literacy* involves some relation to consensus. That is, just as the "Literacy and Culture" students identified *literacy* as some form of sharing similar knowledges, Hirsch suggests that establishing a cultural context of what that shared knowledge must be lends to understanding literacy. The flaw here is that Hirsch too boldly offers a particular collection of what that context is: one that we recognize as inscribing a dominant narrative in order to define what *culture* is and what one must know in order to be literate within that culture. Certainly, the imposition of *any* predetermined "contexts" would be equally oppressive; deciding what is and is not to be included suggests that value may be defined over various cultural knowledges and leads toward hierarchies and oppression. However, despite Hirsch's bold maneuver to define *American culture*, Hirsch's theories do hold particularly intriguing understandings about knowledge making. For instance, while few would not find Hirsch's appendix to *Cultural Literacy: What Every American Needs to Know*, "What Literate Americans Know"—promoted in some editions as "the Thinking American's List"—insulting and oppressive, his overall view of "cultural literacy" suggests the same idea about literacy that many other scholars also promote: consensus. While many who discuss literacy and ideology have come to recognize that grounding foundational definitions of what culture or literacy is may be difficult, most would agree that in order for communication or culture to work there must be shared, similar knowledges. Hirsch is simply saying the same thing in a much more aggravating way. He argues that in order for an individual to participate "literately" in culture that individual must be attuned to a particular body of knowledge that others also share. This is not inaccurate. While I would not go so far as to say that we need to define these cultural contexts as Hirsch does, we do, in fact, regularly devise similar codifications for knowledge that are not as rigid or as unchanging as Hirsch's but are organized contexts none the less. For instance, when we speak for or against "academic discourse" we are talking about a particular cultural context; when we speak about a particular culture, we are speaking about a particular list of shared ideologies and knowledges; when we speak about composition, about Jewish cooking, about fishing, about feminisms, about film, about Power Rangers, about rap music, about Latino/a poetry, about whatever we speak or write, we are drawing on a context, a body of knowledge. However, we recognize, unlike Hirsch, that these contexts can never be codified, defined, or stagnant (Hirsch also acknowledges a need for change). Cultural contexts transform; communication, knowledge making and sharing, thought, discourse all insist that lists be transformative. We have come to recognize that no culture, no body of knowledge, is more valuable than any other, that cultures interact with other cultures, that contexts morph into new conditions, that bodies of knowledge splinter and change. Nonetheless, cultural literacy can be seen in terms of metaphoric lists. We *do* ask students to learn to manipulate contexts and move from one to the next in order to get along in the world just as we move from our daily contexts of composition literacy to our familial contexts of home life and so on. Cultural contexts are already in place, though that place is static. In other words, while we readily—and perhaps correctly—dismiss Hirsch's application of how he wishes to impose cultural literacy, we need not dismiss the theoretical underpinnings to this understanding of literacy and how they help us understand knowledge making.

LITERACY AND LIBERATORY LEARNING

Since compositionists, and educators in general, have begun to recognize the ways in which ideology and literacy affect teaching and learning, new pedagogical approaches have evolved alongside scholarly conversations about literacy and ideology. Frequently labeled "radical pedagogy" or "liberatory learning," a variety of pedagogical approaches has grown from the work of third-world literacy scholars, particularly that of Paulo Freire. Liberatory learning specialists such as Freire are concerned with giving students critical skills such as reading and writing so as to allow them a better opportunity to move from under whatever oppressive force burdens them. That is, Freire and others are concerned with education and literacy as it pertains to the masses of poor, uneducated people in underdeveloped nations whose illiteracy leads to their exploitation. Liberatory learning specialists seek to develop pedagogies that give these masses the tools that will allow them to be critical of their oppressors and in turn free themselves from oppression; in other words, one goal of radical pedagogy is to help students become "critically conscious" of their world.

Freire's work is particularly influential in composition because it offers a view of pedagogy that subverts traditional methods of education through its dialogic and empowering techniques. Freire's goal is to allow students to become full participants in their own education. He does not want students to be turned into "containers" or "receptacles" that teachers try to fill with information. In this model of education, "The more completely [the teacher] fills the receptacles, the better teacher he is. The more meekly the receptacles permit themselves to be filled, the better students they are" (Freire, *Pedagogy* 58). In this model, Freire argues, "the more completely [students] accept the passive role imposed on them, the more they tend simply to adapt to the world as it is and to the fragmented view of reality deposited in them" (60). That is, banking methods of education do not allow students to develop the critical consciousness that would "result from their intervention in the world as transformers of that world" (60).

Freire argues that people are denied the opportunity to develop agency because of social positioning. For Freire, inherent in agency is the ability to think critically and take action in the world; denying agency and action for those who are "illiterate" oppresses and dehumanizes them. The struggle to regain agency, to regain humanity, is for Freire "man's vocation." But Freire stresses that dominant classes cannot free oppressed classes; the oppressed must free themselves. As Irene Ward puts it, "The dominant class cannot bestow freedom or knowledge on the masses as a gift; this only results in false generosity and does not allow people to overcome dependency" (94–95). Hence, part of Freire's pedagogy is a call for transformation of the social structure that will occur as the masses become critically conscious of how social systems act as oppressor. Once the masses can become critically aware of the forces that oppress them, they can begin to actively alter those forces. Thus, the role of radical pedagogies is not to offer students a body of true knowledge but rather to give students an opportunity to view their world critically and, in turn, the opportunity to act in that world.

Drawing on these basic assumptions of agency and action, many educators have seen radical pedagogies as a means by which not only to "educate" students but also to liberate them. That is to say, many see liberatory learning as giving students the opportunity to have voice in how and what they learn, in how they view the world, and in how they live and interact in that world. As we have come to recognize the powerful role that ideology plays in traditional banking models of education, liberatory learning's ideal has come to be seen as a possible avenue by which to subvert—or at least to disrupt—traditional oppressive education and allow students a glimpse of the ideologies that control how and what they learn. Or, as Ward puts it, "Freire's pedagogy is an attempt to break down the traditional educational hierarchy so as to enable students to become full participants in the educational process" (97).

Because compositionists have come to recognize the revolutionary qualities of radical pedagogy, scholars in composition have incorporated the new understanding of ideology and literacy in both theoretical and pedagogical discussions. Perhaps more than any other theory that has been brought to composition, liberatory learning is seen as offering immediate practical results. Many compositionists have lunged at the opportunity to offer radical pedagogies and justifications for these pedagogies because of their strong ties to classroom practices; that is, the pedagogical imperative is the driving force promoting liberatory learning as one (many?) possible approach(es?) to understanding literacy and to addressing the problems of literacy in the classroom. At the same time, the ideals of liberatory learning perhaps help answer the identity crisis—mentioned by Bizzell in one of my epigraphs—that compositionists face in trying to understand what we do toward the common good beyond merely teaching students to get commas in the right place. Radical pedagogy affords compositionists the opportunity to teach more than "the basics"; it allows teachers to move toward returning students the agency of which traditional education robbed them—an admirable and necessary endeavor, indeed.

COMPOSITION AND
RADICAL PEDAGOGY

Like most of the theories that come to composition, Freire's theory of radical pedagogy creates tensions when converted from theory to practice. Freire himself repeatedly emphasizes that he wants to avoid the wholesale transferal of his methods to contexts other than those for which they were designed: the education of non-literate poor people in Brazil. Freire argues that his approaches cannot simply be imported into any context without first exploring that context and then altering the radical pedagogy theories to fit that context. That is, Freire seems to be arguing that local knowledge must determine how pedagogical theory can be applied and that while theory may be applicable to practice local context must determine how the larger theory applies.

Despite these warnings from Freire, many compositionists have eagerly jumped at the opportunity to bring the theoretical framework of Freire's methods to composition classrooms. For instance, Ira Shor, who has worked closely with Freire (so closely, in fact, that Ward claims that no one in composition has criticized his work to see if it is in any way actually Freirean) has had great impact on composition's encounter with Freirean liberatory learning. In *Critical Teaching and Everyday Life*, Shor argues that Freire's liberatory learning can be applied to North American students since they too are similar to Freire's oppressed peasants in that they have been victimized by a system of banking education. Ward argues that Shor sees American students as having become "habituated to passivity by a host of educational practices that more often than not privilege conformity and an unquestioning acceptance of authority" (103).

In order for Shor to accomplish his goal of helping students overcome their alienation from their world and from learning, his pedagogy develops around "pieces of experience." In other words, Shor argues that the theme of a composition class should be something that is relevant to the lives of students: hamburgers or sex, for instance. His pedagogical agenda in doing so is intended to give students "take-away literacy modes" that they can later use without guidance from a teacher; self-reliance and the ability to survive and learn without teachers is central to Shor's pedagogy. Through prewriting and dictation strategies, Shor tries to guide students to make connections between their oral language skills—skills he identifies as already being acquired—and written language skills that they need to acquire. Through a variety of assignments in which students are asked to write about "the worst teacher I ever had," "what is a bad teacher," and "the worst job I ever had," Shor introduces *voicing*, a technique he identifies as "a self-editing tool which calls on students to use the natural grammar in their speaking voices" (133). That is, Shor wants students to recognize that their spoken voices can translate to a written voice and that they have agency in their written work as well as in their oral discourse. He wants students to engage in discourse that has impact on their lives rather than on mere assignments teachers use to fulfill writing requirements. He wants, it seems, to teach students, as Freire describes his own pedagogical theory, to move from reflection and action.

However, Ward criticizes Shor's appropriation of Freirean liberatory learning, citing it as an example of "how Freirean theory can be misused" (104). Ward censures Shor for what seems to be a flaw in his pedagogy: while he wants to provide students with the opportunity to move beyond the passivity of traditional education, his pedagogies—which at first appear to be liberating—still dictate what students can discuss and learn: hamburgers or sex, for example. Shor does not afford students the opportunity to make actual critical and evaluative decisions and judgments about how and what they learn; rather, he determines what *he* sees as relevant to students' lives and imposes those values on his students as he asks them to come to terms with hamburgers or sex. That is, Shor does not place any larger context around his assignments that would allow students to participate in discourse about hamburgers or sex beyond the classroom; his pedagogy is still constrained by the classroom and teacher-student hierarchies. Freire repeatedly points out that any pedagogical approach that does not allow students to move beyond the classroom—what he calls *action*—simply reinscribes traditional banking education and does not lead to liberation. This is not to say that Freire would argue that his theories are not applicable in classrooms; in fact, quite the opposite seems apparent: these theories inherently call the will to pedagogy to the fore. That is, radical pedagogy theories depend on movement toward practice, movement toward action, in order for them to operate. Unlike some poststructural, feminist, or philosophical theories that do not necessarily need practical development for validation, radical pedagogy does need contexts of application in order to function. Shor, however, moves toward application by rewriting Freirean theory to suit his needs and in doing so undermines the original intention of that theory. Hence, movement to classroom practice can be seen here not as a validation of theory, but as a distortion of that theory.

What this indicates is that Freirean liberatory learning—like many other theories that are imported into composition pedagogy—cannot be translated as a wholesale theory; it is difficult to *do* liberatory learning theory. It is condescending for us to take Freire's theory and simply *apply* it to North American students; they are not peasants, and they do not "lack" in the same ways that Freire's peasants do. In addition, those who bring liberatory learning to North American classrooms—Shor, for instance—do so in a prescriptive manner. Most scholars who write about radical pedagogies for composition classes (and for other North American classes, too) tend to have a "vision" of what these theories should accomplish in their classrooms. That is, many who promote radical pedagogy as an answer to the "literacy crisis" and as a means of bringing students to critical consciousness seem to have an end in sight for their classrooms. Through a promotion of "critical thinking," teachers seem to appropriate the very agency they claim to wish to return to students by prescribing a particular set of values as to what and how students should think "critically." They have a particular goal in mind for their students—a particular goal *they* have decided is necessary for their students to achieve and a particular way that *they* see as the appropriate way to think. Many who import liberatory learning are merely finding new ways to appropriate thinking, ideology, and epistemology and inscribing those of the educator under the guise of liberation. This is very different from Freire's ethnographic model in which literacy workers study a culture prior to determining how and what should be taught.

In many ways, when Freirean liberatory learning is translated into composition pedagogies—as in Shor's case—educators still create categories in the "I know/you don't know" game; here, however, the categories seem to be the "we" who can bequeath critical consciousness and the "they" who *need* to have it thrust upon them. In bringing radical pedagogical theory to the composition classroom (or to any other classroom, for that matter) by simply importing the theories without considering the context in which they were devised, we deny a major facet of those theories: that educators have traditionally already done the same thing under headings other than *liberatory*. When we take an ethical position similar to the one Bizzell posits in promoting the "values that we cherish," we assume that these are the values that all should cherish, and, in turn, we use our classroom authority—which is always present—to inscribe these values where we assume they are the same values others have or should have.[5] That is to say, when we attempt to import radical pedagogy theories to North American classrooms, in many ways we reinscribe systems of stratification by implying that we are able to teach access to power, since we already have a privileged knowledge of that power and we have licensed ability to give access to that power.

In any case, perhaps one of the dangers of "translating" radical pedagogical theory into practice is that, as with some feminist theory, it becomes neutralized and appropriated as it encounters composition. That is, as with other theories that make their way into composition, composition or, more specifically, certain compositionists manipulate those theories so as not to allow their original agendas to be fulfilled. Just as Shor and others actually reinscribe banking education under the guise of Freirean liberatory learning and he and others prescribe their vision to students, so too do other theories become offset by rigid traditions of composition pedagogy. Perhaps it is precisely this difficult intersection between theory and practice—even theories such as radical pedagogies that are seen as classroom theories—that lead us to think beyond classroom strategies to the larger role of how we think about literacy, ideology, and learning. That is, as we find difficulty coming to terms with how we actually *liberate* students in our classrooms, we begin to question and argue about our larger role in issues of literacy and how our theoretical and pedagogical conversations lead us to real Freirean action.

GETTING IT RIGHT(?)

While many compositionists have brought liberatory theories to composition classrooms in ways that do not serve to liberate, Eleanor Kutz and Hephzibah Roskelly's *An Unquiet Pedagogy: Transforming Practice in the English Classroom* is perhaps one of the more effective introductions of Freire's theories into North American composition classrooms. In his foreword to the text, Freire writes that he is pleased to see that Kutz and Roskelly do not appropriate a how-to importation of his theories without considering local context. He argues that *An Unquiet Pedagogy* demonstrates "a profound understanding that practices and experiences can be neither imported nor exported. In essence, Kutz and Roskelly have liberated themselves from the North American culture of how-to manuals" (ix). He contends that Kutz and Roskelly have appropriately "extracted the valid principles" of his theories "so they could be re-created and reinvented in the North American context" (ix). He writes that by

> understanding and emphasizing the role of language in cul-tural and multicultural literacies, Kutz and Roskelly have, in a significant way, advanced the theoretical discourse that views students' language as the only means by which they can develop their own voice. It is through their own lan-guage that they will be able to reconstruct their history and their culture, hence their position in the world. (ix)

Kutz and Roskelly argue that American schools have developed their structures in response to a "variety of social and economic fac-tors" which traditionally isolated teachers from students and teachers from other teachers (8–9). More recently in classrooms, however, cultural and social factors have begun to create more isolation: class-rooms are filled with students from multiple cultural backgrounds who have various ways of knowing, of communicating, of learning. Many education critics—Kutz and Roskelly specify E. D. Hirsch as an example—see this diversity as contributing to the decline of the qual-ity of American education. Yet Kutz and Roskelly see this very diversity as central to helping students "achieve the kind of higher literacy that society now demands and it can help to create a different and more effective relationship among the cultures of the home, of the school, and of the larger society" (10). Kutz and Roskelly set out to explore various "strands of learning" that a teacher might "bring to her teaching, weaving them into a coherent understanding of what constitutes truly literate behavior, of the ways in which language, cognition, reading, and writing work together in the classroom, and of how they are affected by culture and society" (10).

Recognizing teaching *and* learning as active endeavors in which teachers, learners, readers, and writers "*act* rather than react in the classroom," Kutz and Roskelly promote a relationship "between teachers and learners as individuals and as part of culture and believe that classrooms build and expand ways of knowing by using the rela-tionship between individuals and community and culture" (10–11). That is, the relationship between students and teachers—between Kutz and Roskelly and their readers—is interactive:

> Teaching must be *unquiet* in both senses of that word. There must be talk—lots of it—among administrators, parents,

teachers, students, the community and the culture at large.
And there must be change—true change—that comes from
individuals' becoming critically aware of the many factors
that shape the school. Only when pedagogy is unquiet does it
have a chance to make a difference in the real lives of students and teachers alike. (12)

For Kutz and Roskelly, part of this activity is breaking from a tradition wherein students ask questions of their teachers but teachers
rarely question their own learning. Throughout the text, Kutz and
Roskelly offer various strategies that encourage teachers to learn and
inquire about their classrooms along with their students. They suggest teachers keep journals about their classrooms and engage in
ethnographic studies of their classrooms in order to learn not more
about their students per se but about themselves as teachers. Part of
this inquiry asks teachers to explore the relationship between "what
students know and what they express" (33).

Kutz and Roskelly argue that "despite the fact that people learn in
more than one way and know things through more than one means,
our schools have, by and large, allowed just one way of knowing to
be developed in the classroom, an analytical and discrete way, often
competitive and individualistic, highly abstract and intellectualized,
and authority-centered" (50). This traditional way of teaching/learn-
ing, they argue, leaves students and teachers little room in which to
"explore, inquire, question, or create abstractions from their own
experiences" (50). That is, traditional learning and teaching serve to
silence students in their classrooms. They contend that students and
teachers alike need to learn not to ignore exactly what each brings to
the classroom.

In terms of writing pedagogy in particular, Kutz and Roskelly
argue that learners acquire the most important language skills
"unconsciously in an environment that provides rich data" (135).
That is, they posit that traditional memorization of grammar skills
will not teach students to write better. They offer useful ways in
which teachers can help students come to terms with their grammar
"errors" in the context of their writing rather than in terms of "rules."
They suggest that teachers encourage students to "ignore the errors"
since as they read and write they will acquire those skills; learn to see
if students understand the principle behind particular constructions;
explicitly explain grammar to students when they ask; let students
edit each other's work and learn to explain grammar to each other;
stop teaching by means of emphasizing error; recognize that there

are more crucial areas to focus on than students' grammar errors (134–35). Like many of the other "strategies" that Kutz and Roskelly offer, their approaches to grammar reexamine ways in which traditional educational systems have taught students. By encouraging teachers to recognize the locality, the relevance, the context of grammar in students' writing, Kutz and Roskelly push for a much more individualized, culturally centered, local form of writing instruction. Granted, my use of their grammar example might seem to trivialize writing instruction in the larger scheme of the liberatory agenda they forward, but it seems that when their pedagogy finds a means by which to radically rethink what has traditionally been labeled as a critical and generally memorizable aspect of writing—an aspect that we have come to recognize as trivial in the larger scope of the function of writing—then perhaps this pedagogy begins to transcend typical radical pedagogical agendas of liberating students and to offer a means by which both to liberate and actually help students to learn about writing and discourse.

Despite Kutz and Roskelly's admirable attempt to find ways to bring liberatory learning to composition classrooms in more effective pedagogies, pedagogies perhaps more representative of the theories from which they derived, Kutz and Roskelly, like so many other compositionists, fall prey to the prejudice that these theories must transform into effective pedagogies. In their chapter "Theory into Practice," the authors acknowledge that "'how do you do it?' is always an important question for teachers, and too much of a teacher's preparation in universities has left out that essential component" (247). They explain that

> English courses have taught subject matter and education courses have taught pedagogical methods, but for most teachers the two have never met in an integrated theoretical and practical approach to classroom instruction. This is one reason some teachers are resentful of theory: it's all very well to spell out what's needed, but sometimes a very different matter to put any of it to work productively in an actual classroom in a real school. (247)

Like other scholars seeking validation of theory through practice, Kutz and Roskelly adamantly see a need for practical affirmation. What makes this example of the pedagogical imperative problematic is that the theories they seek to authenticate through pedagogy are, to a great extent, pedagogical theories. Granted, a good deal of

The Unquiet Pedagogy addresses the theoretical reasons for implementing liberatory pedagogies, but the culminating goal of the work is to provide practical approaches to these theories. Yet, unlike much of the prejudice against theory that seeks validation through practical application, application in this scenario seems necessary. It is silly, at this point, for me to argue that even pedagogical theory can stand on its own without practical application. I believe that more than any other theory brought to composition studies, liberatory learning theories stand to gain not necessarily from direct translation into practice without local consideration—as Shor seems to do—but from examination of those theories and localized application. However, this is not to say that Freirean liberatory learning does not also offer theoretical understandings of ideology, culture, and discourse that necessarily need pedagogical applications to help us better understand their operations.

Like the many other theories that come to composition, literacy theories stand to offer substantial information regarding the social aspects of discourse. However, unlike many other theories, they also have the potential to more readily influence classroom practices since a good deal of these theories evolve as responses to classroom needs. Perhaps these theories have become more immediately accepted by compositionists because they answer the call to pedagogy more directly than other theories of discourse.

6

CONTINUING THE
THEORY DEBATES

"I had entered a new knowledge or allowed it to enter
me, a circumstance that requires an act of relaxation, a
surrender, a submission to the knowledge one wishes to
possess."

— *Howell Raines,* Fly Fishing
Through the Midlife Crisis

"I brood over the problem of where the possible connections lie, passing threads of thought through my mind in
much the way that fishermen, the world over, from
Galilee to Tidewater, pass the strands of a net through
their hands looking, not for connections, but for discon-
nections, the holes to be repaired."

— *James Britton, foreword to* Rhetorical Traditions
and the Teaching of Writing

As I have examined the ways in which composition
and particular theories—poststructural, postprocess, feminist, and
literacy—engage one another, I have become engrossed by Lynn Worsham's identification of the "pedagogical imperative" and the "will to
pedagogy" (96). Worsham correctly identifies an overwhelming voice
in composition that has come to validate theory only through its
implications for immediate classroom application. Certainly, we can
see why; daily, compositionists face what David Bleich would call
"real" classroom problems. And for compositionists such as Bleich
and others, theoretical inquiry that does not contribute to immediate
"use" in facing these problems is of little use for "real" compositionists. Yet, as I have examined ways in which this prejudice against
theory has rejected many important theories, I have also become conscious that this prejudice is irrational and potentially destructive to
the advancement of the discipline of rhetoric and composition.

In the preceeding pages, I have tried to demonstrate not only ways
in which theory is resisted in composition but also ways in which the
very theories that many resist actually benefit our understanding of

the operation of discourse. Perhaps what has become most clear to me is the continued need to speculate, observe, mirror, consider, analyze, and engage in all of the other activities that the term *theorize* suggests. For ages, knowledge that has been determined through such methods has been deemed superior because of its universal quality; yet critics now charge such knowledge as ignoring local context. I hope to have demonstrated that despite the anti-theory positions taken for whatever reason—theory fear, pedagogical imperative, anti-intellectualism, and so on—theorizing has led composition to challenge orthodoxies that limited its borders in the academy to a service position for teaching mechanical skills of "getting it right." Rather, we have come to recognize, through theory, that composition instruction involves much more; discourse, we have learned, is much more than a series of rules for where commas belong.

Through compositionists who bring theory to composition, we have come to recognize that how we teach, what we teach, how our students learn, and what our students learn are dependent on forces beyond our control. Through the theoretical works of theorists outside of composition such as Michel Foucault, Donald Davidson, Richard Rorty, Hélène Cixous, and many others, we have restructured how we view the role of composition and communication. Since I have already examined how compositionists engage many of the theories that have led to these changes, I would like to explain why I see these theories as having the most impact on the shifting identity of composition as a field. Of many theories that have begun to work their way into composition, perhaps the overriding assumption that stands to continually alter our vision of composition is that of the social and ideological understanding of composition.

In recent years, the composition textbook market has been overwhelmed by texts that push toward a thematic focus that we label "multicultural" or "diverse." For numerous theoretical reasons, our discussions of pedagogy have begun to emphasize our understanding of discourse as social enterprise. Certainly, this understanding grows from theoretical positions that evolved from within and from outside of practical classroom experience as well as from practitioners' discussions of classroom needs and operations. Nonetheless, over time, we have come to recognize a new "vision" of what composition *is*.

Perhaps it is this new "vision" that has brought so much critique of theoretical speculation to the fore. No longer are bastions of truth available to scholars who look longingly to past days when knowing what a "compositionist" was supposed to do was as simple as knowing a few grammar rules. Part of the resistance to theory (such as Bleich's) may come from an understanding that literacy (and composition) is vastly different from what their "knowledge" tells them it is. With the introduction of new literacies—e.g., computer literacy—fear of the new curriculum may be exhibited as a resistance to theory that pushes composition toward new, unfamiliar knowledges. It is particularly these new knowledges, new understandings of composition, of discourse, that lead us to question the future of composition.

WHERE ARE WE GOING?

In 1966 at the now famous Anglo-American Seminar on Teaching and Learning of English at Dartmouth College, James Britton argued "that we cannot define English by defining its subject matter. Rather, we must first ask what the function of English is in the curriculum and in the lives of students" (qtd. in Harris 141). As Joseph Harris explains, Britton was not interested in how the "subject matter" of English was to be defined but instead in "what we want our students to do" (141). That is, as Harris argues, "Britton believed that any map of the subject was bound to be an interested and partial one, an argument for a particular sort of methods, aims and practices" (141).

Just as Britton and Albert Kitzhaber conflicted over the answer to the question "What is English?" at the Dartmouth Conference, so composition is engaged in a debate regarding the future role of the discipline. On the one hand, theorists have begun to regard rhetoric and composition as an intellectual endeavor that extends beyond mere grammar-school "basics," while many on the other side of the argument see composition as a strictly service-oriented field. Like Kitzhaber and Britton's debate, at stake is not the accuracy of theory but the need for many to know how or if particular theories affect the curriculum and what teachers and students do in composition classrooms. In essence, at issue is the value of the speculative nature of theory versus the usefulness of the action that speculation may produce. To a certain degree, the need to validate theory in practice asks that theories be seen in black and white terms of true or false—theories that can be applied and theories that cannot.

Yet as new theories have been questioned and have come to the fore—some regarded as immediately applicable to composition classrooms and others not—many theories have redefined composition, our understanding of pedagogy, and our understanding of discourse. Currently, theories of culture, race, ethnicity, class, gender, and other "social issues" have greatly redirected our vision of "what composition is." No longer do many composition classrooms seek to delineate a particular set of axioms to define appropriate discourse and appropriate writing. Rather, we have come to recognize that the inscription of such narratives would be oppressive and would simply reinscribe dominant discourse. Instead, we have become conscious of the heteroglossia in our classrooms, and we have attempted to account for the multiple knowledges which students bring to the composition classroom.

It seems that as we contend with new theories of how race, class, gender, ethnicity, and other social issues impact composition classrooms, the "new curriculum" will move beyond the traditional service orientation from which many compositionists are steering. Theoretical and practical inquiry regarding the role of social issues and discourse present radical challenges to orthodoxies within composition. Issues regarding difference have enabled composition to become an interdisciplinary field and have reframed our understanding of discourse so that we might become more conscious of the complexity of what we do as composition teachers. Through a commitment to examining the role of all discourse in larger schemes of everyday life, composition has taken on the new role of teaching students not just to "get it right" but also to find agency in their worlds. Like Patricia Bizzell's argument that we have moved toward doing so in composition to help fill a need for reasons of fulfillment, composition has pushed to gain an ethical commitment to helping students find agency.

We have come to recognize that the actions of educators have—whether consciously or not—had powerfully suppressive effects. Through speculation into various explanations of why and how the teaching of discourse has had these effects, we began to greatly alter the role of composition teachers and the role of composition in the academy. But we have done so only through careful speculation, questioning, and requestioning. The conventional wisdom of the discipline has shifted tremendously in the past thirty years. Composition has embraced and rejected multiple theories, but while many have sought the one panacea theory or practice, composition has become a complicated field that cannot rely on a single theory or a comprehensive pedagogy to answer all of the questions that arise in classrooms or in scholarly inquiry as to the nature of discourse. The retrieval and legitimation of knowledge in composition studies has grown complicated and exciting, and we are far from reaching decisive conclusions. Continued debate over the field's controversies must proliferate as the ever-growing breadth of composition pushes the discipline to new identities. As the borders of composition studies expand and become blurred, mingling with those of fields such as linguistics, anthropology, sociology, the "hard sciences," and the many other codified "subjects," composition "experts" are going to have to become more conscious of the multifaceted aspects of their field; theorizing about those facets will certainly help the evolution of composition.

There is little question that the issue of *theory* in composition has been greatly called into question. Stanley Fish, one of theory's most outspoken critics has warned, "Theory's day is dying" ("Consequences" 128). Criticism from various sources including the neo-pragmatists, postmodernists, anti-intellectuals, and particularly compositionists who advocate practice over theory has begun to polarize knowledge making in composition. Steven Knapp and Walter Benn Michaels argue that "no one can reach a position outside practice, that theorists should stop trying, and that theoretical enterprise should therefore come to an end" (30). I would argue that doing so in an evolving discipline such as composition would serve to stagnate a growing field. Yet similar sentiments proliferate from within composition and from without (see Chapter One).

And so the question remains, Where are we going? As I mentioned early on, I do not intend to resolve any theory debates. Doing so would be counterproductive, would stand to stagnate composition, and would serve to inscribe a particular set of values. Rather, I am probably going to leave more questions unanswered than those with which I began. Yet I do see a particular direction in which composition is moving via these theory debates: one of cultural, social recognition both of classroom activity and theoretical inquiry. Furthermore, by way of the many competing theories that come to composition—and the many arguments that extend from them—composition has evolved into one of the most exciting disciplines in the academy. Because composition has become a meeting ground of theories, it is becoming a truly interdisciplinary field. And so I answer my question by saying, "We are going everywhere."

Rhetoric and composition is rapidly becoming more attuned to discourses other than just specifically written (academic) discourse. As we have come to recognize academic discourse as simply another site—instead of a "correct" discourse—we have learned to teach academic discourse as convention just as we have learned to teach technical writing, argumentation, persuasion, narration, or exposition as convention. And we have learned to do so through theorizing. If I were to ask, "What theories are useful?" I would have to answer in a riddling manner much like a character from *Alice in Wonderland* or even Tolkien's Gollum: all and none. That is, all of the theories have in some way or another altered our understanding of discourse, and none has given us full understanding of it. So the question seems to me to be, What do we do with theory?

THEORY, THEORY, THEORY

As I have argued in Chapter One, many anti-foundational reactions against theory conclude that there is no longer any reason for "doing theory," and pro-practice critics of theory argue that unless it is possible to "do theory" a particular theory is of little consequential value. However, such arguments deny the beneficial quality of theory and deny the positive impact theory has had on composition studies. Joseph Harris correctly points out that "theory cannot provide us with a neutral foundation of knowledge from which we can then derive correct methods of reading, writing, and teaching. But it can offer a way of arguing about (and perhaps changing) the things we do and believe as teachers and intellectuals" (144). That is, theory has the ability not necessarily to offer concrete practices based on particular theories, but theory can influence various aspects of how we think about teaching *and* how we think about composition as a body of knowledge.

Yet for Harris and the theorists he turns to in support of this argument (Stephen Mailloux and Gerald Graff), "such views of theory do not privilege it as a base or ground of understanding, as something separate from and prior to practice" (144). That is, placing theory and practice in binary opposition—to say, "this is theory; this is not"—is not possible since the two are so enmeshed that they become indistinguishable at points. Yet I would argue that while it is impossible to identify a practice that has not evolved from or been altered by theory, theory can exist without practical applications. Theory can, as I have shown, offer important insights into the operation of discourse. However, in composition, for the most part, theories are privileged, rejected, criticized, embraced, or shown as interesting only when they are directly coupled with practice. As C. H. Knoblauch and Lil Brannon explain in *Rhetorical Traditions and the Teaching of Writing*, "Teachers have their hands full just doing their jobs day by day without taking on the added burden of theoretical hardware. New teachers especially find Monday morning an urgent, looming reality, and they need practical information to cope with it" (1). Yet while Knoblauch and Brannon openly display the prejudice that theory is valued only when grounded in practice, they do not sympathize with teachers who do not acknowledge the role theory plays in the development of the Monday morning practice:

> The trouble is, we can't extend the same sympathy to certain assumptions underlying a restrictively practical viewpoint: the assumption, for example, that teachers can be purposeful and effective while remaining unconscious of the intellectual motivations supporting their work; or the assumption that all classroom activities reflect identical arguments about how people write and learn to write, so that choosing among them is a matter of personal taste in the context of equally legitimate alternatives; or the assumption that any one teaching practice can be joined with any other without effecting the coherence or quality of instruction. (1–2)

Certainly, Knoblauch and Brannon have begun to make the connection between the importance of theory and the evolution of composition. However, inherent in their understanding of the relationship between theory and composition is that *composition* involves practice and that grounding theory in that practice is the only means of validation of particular theories. That is, despite their conscious effort to promote theoretical awareness, they are restricted to the validation-by-practice prejudice that engulfs composition. Even as they bring theory to the fore in defining what it means to be "philosophical"—that is, theoretical—they do so in terms of practice:

> What does it mean to be "philosophical" about the teaching of writing? In general, it means being aware of what one is doing and why. It includes having an exploratory and reflective attitude toward ideas, issues, and questions pertinent to how people write and how they develop as writers. It means observing writers' actual practices as the test of plausible generalizations about what composing involves and how it occurs. It means speculating about the significance of what is observed in order to enhance or revise earlier conclusions. It means applying personal conclusions to the larger conversation about writing and teaching that is going on today in professional journals and conferences—and that has been going on for centuries. It means teaching from sound conceptual premises

that are understood, consciously sustained, and continually modified in light of new knowledge about composing and accumulated experience in the classroom. (2)

Knoblauch and Brannon are conscious of the role and operation of theory; they ask teachers to participate in the furthering of theory—a necessary endeavor. However, like many compositionists, such speculation serves to promote improved practice as its sole goal. That is, despite their promotion of theoretical inquiry, Knoblauch and Brannon do so solely for practical gain.

Similar to Knoblauch and Brannon's goal of helping practitioners become more aware of the important role of theory, Lee Odell's collection *Theory and Practice in the Teaching of Writing: Rethinking the Discipline* is intended to help "take an active role in shaping and reshaping the theories that underlie our daily practice as writers and as teachers of writing" (1). For Odell and others, theory *does* play an important role in composition, and he criticizes the opponents of theory for not giving a complete account of theory:

They don't consider some of the strong reasons we have for believing that theory is implicit in everything we do, in our routine work as writers and teachers as well as in major developments in our discipline. Moreover, the critics of theory don't help us understand that theory and practice are interactive, each capable of informing and remaking the other. (2)

Here, the language is clear: theory *and* practice are significant to the evolution of the discipline, and critics of theory deny a crucial aspect of that relationship. As Odell argues, "theory often figures prominently in efforts to bring about fundamental changes in practice" (though, I would say "always figures prominently") (2). Yet, as Odell explores how particular theories have been imported into composition, the overriding theme of *theory into practice* still persists. In his title, Odell calls for a "rethinking" of the discipline, but this rethinking comes in the traditional way—as his title implies—of linking "theory and practice" together.

Perhaps these two examples should suffice in making this point, but as I look over the titles of books in composition from the past fifteen years, I see that this link between theory *and* practice has been a recurring theme. This connection between theory and practice has been, and should continue to be, critical to the evolution of the discipline. However, even as many scholars and teachers are willing to make this connection, many are also eager to dispel the need for theory that doesn't lend to this connection. In Chapter One, I argue that daily we are forced to participate in practice and to produce theory that explains the nature, function, and operation of discourse. In doing so, compositionists, whether engaged in theoretical pursuit or consumed by teaching six sections of basic writing, need to explore the ways in which theory from various ideological and epistemological backgrounds influences both the theoretical inquiries and the diurnal practice that makes up the field's bread and butter. Herein lies what I see as "the new curriculum."

It seems that as compositionists engage the theory debates and attempt to define the roles that theory and practice play in composition's development, we must begin to do so in more productive ways. I have shown many of the unproductive attacks on theory (see Chapter One) and many of the ways in which particular theories engage composition (the next four chapters), and in doing so, I have attempted to explore the ways in which contemporary composition informs pedagogy, the ways in which it has been imported into the classroom, its successes and failures, and the potential that theory holds for informing pedagogy. And while none of these pursuits can be concretely answered and we cannot achieve balance in the interaction between theory and composition pedagogy, it is apparent that, as with any other discipline, composition's search for "universal truths" through theoretical speculation has pushed us toward current understandings about discourse. So rather than offer a classroom curriculum based on my observations about "useful" theories—which would be self-defeating—I offer instead a curriculum for scholars and teachers at all levels in composition.

Since theorizing is an attempt to arrive at accurate explanations of a particular phenomenon and in the case of composition that phenomenon—discourse—is often viewed as static, we can assume that no totalizing theory of discourse will be formulated. However, because of the transformative nature of both theory and discourse, composition studies inherently necessitate continued speculation to further the motion of understanding what we can of discourse. That is, it is imperative that as scholars and teachers we speculate further at all levels regarding discourse, whether the analysis of such speculation leads to immediate practical results or not.

In composition, the debate regarding what "body of knowledge" constitutes *rhetoric and composition* dictates that composition maintains no constant, codifiable knowledge. However, as composition has searched for identity among this transformative amalgam of knowledge and within the academy, the theory debates have produced many advances in the field's recent and rapid evolution. Theorizing has pushed us beyond Enlightenment rationality to a more socially based understanding of language and of what it is we do in the academy, in the world (though some would argue that theory *qua* theory *is* a facet Enlightenment rationality). Until we are explicitly able to define that role to our satisfaction, only continued speculation will push us toward a more comprehensive understanding of what rhetoric and composition *is*. That is, we could certainly cease all theoretical speculation and consciously decide that composition studies will forever stand as it does today and that any further understanding of discourse would only hinder the comfort of an unchanging discipline. I shudder to think that if Bleich or Knapp and Michaels or Fish could actually bring an end to theoretical speculation what would become of this field. Besides, just as theory does so much for composition, composition does so much for theory. Because we have very few theories that we can label as true "composition" theories, we have depended upon various fields for supplying us with knowledge, and composition has perhaps done more to further speculation from a variety of disciplinary backgrounds than any other field. This has been as beneficial to theoretical pursuit as it has been to the academy; just as theory changes the academy, "theory often gets modified as it 'travels' through the academy" (Said 226).

FINAL THOUGHTS

Without begging the question, I wish to return to the words of several scholars whom I have cited throughout this project as an attempt at closure; however, in doing so, I in no way want to suggest that there should be closure in the theory debates—only in this entry to that conversation.

James J. Sosnoski sums up much of the frustration many compositionists—practitioners and theorists alike—feel: "Writing is painful. Students hurt. Teachers hurt" (217). But he also summarizes a possible alleviation of that pain: "Postmodern theorizing helps" (217). Gary A. Olson is correct in his assessment that "Theory for theory's sake is *not* an abdication of responsibility; it is *not* necessarily cynical careerism. Rhetoric and composition has become an intellectual discipline; we have an obligation to continue and even expand . . . theoretical scholarship" (Role 5).

I have several times mentioned that ultimately I don't want this conversation to come to consensus; doing so would be unproductive. As I have also said, I am not attempting to solve the theory/practice, theory/anti-theory debates. I am not interested in choosing balance or tension, as I have quoted Gayatri Spivak in Chapter One. I do not want the field to fall into simple codifiable terms of a practice/theory binary in which either theory or practice is privileged; such a vision is misguided. There are issues about writing, about language, about discourse that do not directly impact our daily classroom lives—issues that we as scholars are obligated to explore. Theory does not necessarily have to inform pedagogy. It is the responsibility of the discipline to continue theoretical pursuits, to continue the dialectic between theory and practice, to disallow stagnation in the field, and to keep debating in productive ways.

AFTERWORD

COUNTERING THE
GHOSTS OF THEORY
FEAR AMONG US

GARY A. OLSON

Sidney Dobrin argues that the discipline of rhetoric and composition is much more than the study of effective pedagogical methods; it also encompasses scholarly investigations of all aspects of written discourse. Consequently, it is entirely legitimate—even necessary—that scholars study those features of discourse that may have no apparent connection with the teaching of composition. Thus, this book takes a position in the so-called theory wars that still plague composition in its struggle for identity. As a statement in the debate over the role of theory in composition, *Constructing Knowledges* is eminently well reasoned, cogently argued, and gracefully written.

As with many insightful books, Dobrin's is likely to meet with a certain amount of controversy, for it delves into issues that to some are deeply disturbing. In order to illustrate the kind of ideological perspective that this book attempts to counter, let me provide a brief example. Not so long ago *College English* published a "review essay" on two recently published but very different scholarly monographs: *Small Groups in Writing Workshops: Invitations to a Writer's Life* (by Robert Brooke, Ruth Mirtz, and Rick Evans) and *Literacy, Ideology, and Dialogue: Towards a Dialogic Pedagogy* (by Irene Ward). *Small Groups* is about the authors' pedagogy and is, as the reviewer comments, "grounded in the experience of student writers and teachers." *Literacy* (a book from SUNY Press) is a scholarly text that argues that the concept of dialogism is used uncritically by compositionists from widely divergent intellectual and ideological perspectives as if all of these scholars and teachers conceived of dialogism in the same way; Ward examines exactly *how* dialogism is used by various groups in the field, demonstrating that in fact the concept means very different things to people from competing ideological perspectives (Paulo Freire's dialogue is vastly different from Peter Elbow's—so much so that in effect the same word is being used to signify radically divergent processes.) Thus, Ward devotes separate chapters to how dialogue is used by people from each of several identifiable perspectives in the field, and she ends the text with a chapter that attempts to extract from these competing notions of dialogue those properties that are perhaps most valuable and might lead to a more comprehensive and serviceable notion of dialogue.

Now, it strikes me that Ward's book is an eminently useful kind of treatment of a terribly common but problematic concept in the field, and I believe that by examining the problematic nature of how we use this term (in the same way that Joseph Harris's Braddock Award–winning article examines the problematic nature of the notion of community), Ward has made a substantial contribution to composition scholarship—despite the fact that the text itself is not concerned per se with what to do in the composition classroom on Monday. The *College English* reviewer, however, does not agree.

The most troubling problem is that the reviewer obviously does not understand the thesis of the book (incredibly, she admits in print to "skimming through" the text), reading the book instead as "an extended literature review" and assuming, erroneously, that the whole point of the book is the final chapter which, the reviewer believes, is supposedly establishing a dialogism that she can somehow incorporate into her pedagogy—what she tellingly terms "the real stuff." Despite this egregious misreading, however, what makes this review particularly relevant to the issues that Dobrin explicates in his book is how the reviewer's anti-theoretical—and what some, including Dobrin, would term "anti-intellectual"—perspective infects her ability to perceive the Ward book as the kind of intellectual work we do, or should be doing, in composition.

For example, the author begins the review like this: "I'll admit up front to a bias: I'm partial to practitioner research. I like it when teachers talk about teaching—when they reflect on what they do, why they do it, and what it all means." I like to read such works too, but I certainly would not want to judge all scholarship in the field according to whether it did just that; I don't like red meat but I wouldn't presume to prevent a dinner companion from ordering a rare steak. Given the reviewer's admitted bias, we have to ask why she chose to review the Ward text in the first place; after all, it was her choice, not the editor's. As with any choice we make in life, the reviewer's is a *political* one. The review is a political statement, one maintaining that the only scholarship worth reading is that work directly "reflective" on teaching practice. In fact, she lauds *Small Groups* as "an excellent model of reflective practice," setting that text up as a foil to Ward's.

Incredibly, the reviewer admits that it is "hard for me to be fair" about the Ward text, and she comments that she is growing "more and more impatient lately" with scholarship that is theoretical, "academic," and unconnected to teaching. Aside from the fact that the reviewer completely misses the point of the Ward book and thereby does a great disservice not only to Ward but to those of us who consulted her review to determine whether we ourselves should read the text, this reviewer is participating in the kind of ideological infighting that Dobrin so articulately addresses in *Constructing Knowledges*. Clearly, the ghost of Maxine Hairston and of those who between 1985 and 1990 viciously attacked theoretical scholarship in the field still hovers over our daily work. Even in seemingly innocuous forums such as book reviews, we can detect the "fear of theory," as if theoretical scholarship somehow detracted from rather than enriched our intellectual lives.

Dobrin's vision of the field is one that many of us share. We see rhetoric and composition as an intellectually exciting, interdisciplinary discipline concerned with all aspects of written discourse, including but not limited to investigations into effective pedagogy. Perhaps what troubles people like the *College English* reviewer is the feeling of insecurity that can arise from participating in such a sprawling, expansive field. After all, it may be difficult to feel part of a "community" when some of our colleagues are busy investigating the contributions of the sophists, while others are exploring the value of hypertext, and still others are theorizing how feminist theory may shed light on discourse practices. More certain, clearly demarcated disciplinary boundaries would surely afford us more emotional security, but at what cost?

It has always struck me as counterintuitive, not to mention self-destructive, to argue, often with religious fervor, that because rhetoric and composition is a marginalized field and one devoted exclusively to teaching, any attempt to import "theory" from other disciplines is an attempt to abandon this marginalized status and to denigrate teaching or to deny our students quality instruction. Dobrin's text addresses such positions and goes a long way toward adding much-needed perspective to the debate.

Every compositionist concerned with issues of disciplinary identity and with the role of theory in the field should read Sidney Dobrin's *Constructing Knowledges*. It is a major contribution to our understanding of what rhetoric and composition is—and, more importantly—what it can become.

NOTES

2. POSTMODERNIST THOUGHT AND THE TEACHING OF WRITING

1. Throughout this chapter I use the term *postmodernism* (and its derivatives) to refer to the larger school of thought which seeks to disrupt Enlightenment rationality and traditional intellectual and epistemological hegemonies. From time to time, however, I specifically refer to a facet of postmodernism known as *poststructuralism*. In these instances—while *postmodernism* still applies as a more encompassing term—I refer specifically to those theories that have evolved as a response to structuralist ideas: that it is possible to "understand" the order and operation of phenomena (frequently referred to as *text*) by constructing reliable models, or what Foucault calls the "principle of unity." Thus, poststructuralism is a critique of the structuralist attempt to identify the universal underlying structure of phenomena.

2. Obviously, my glossing here of Berlin and Bizzell does not do justice to their important contributions to the integration of poststructuralist theory (particularly that pertaining to the social) into composition. And, in fact, their positions are not purely postmodern in that they are informed by numerous other discourses such as radical pedagogy. For a thorough look at Bizzell's discussions of critical consciousness, see *Academic Discourse and Critical Consciousness*; see also Berlin's "Rhetoric and Ideology in the Writing Class."

3. This discussion, as in my treatment of Berlin and Bizzell, calls for recognition of Paulo Freire's influence. I discuss Freire's work and influence in Chapter Five.

3. POSTPROCESS THEORY AND THE PEDAGOGICAL IMPERATIVE

1. See, for instance, Bleich or Hairston.

2. Rorty is not alone in making this claim. There seems to be a large movement in many disciplines to understand knowledge in various academic discourses as narrative. See, for instance, Donna Harraway in the sciences and Clifford Geertz in anthropology.

3. Kent's rethinking of our rhetorical tradition begins with the pre-Socratic sophistic tradition and moves through time to encompass such a wide berth of scholarship that Kent admits it to be too grand a task to attempt, although he does offer a closer look at the Sophists (see "Paralogic"). But since this discussion does not directly tie to his assessment of composition pedagogy, I will not pursue this important aspect of his critique here.

4. See, for instance, Sharon Crowley's description of who actually writes in writing classrooms (35–36).

5. Sanchez borrows this term from Victor Vitanza.

6. My criticisms of Sanchez's pedagogy were first voiced in response to his CCCC paper in my presentation "Problems of Translating Dialogic Theories into Advanced Composition Pedagogy."

7. For thorough discussions of anti-foundationalism and composition pedagogy, see Bizzell's "Cognition, Convention, and Certainty: What We Need to Know about Writing," "Foundationalism and Anti-Foundationalism in Composition Studies," "Beyond Anti-Foundationalism to Rhetorical Authority: Problems Defining 'Cultural Literacy,'" and Faigley's *Fragments of Rationality: Postmodernity and the Subject of Composition.* Also, see Fish for response to anti-foundational pedagogies.

8. *JAC: A Journal of Composition Theory* (formerly *Journal of Advanced Composition*), *College Composition and Communication,* and *Rhetoric Review.*

4. FEMINIST THEORY AND ITS INTERACTION WITH COMPOSITION PEDAGOGY

1. Certain feminists argue that men cannot participate in feminist conversations as true feminists. I recognize the limited male perspective from which I can speak of feminism but do so as a compositionist who must and wishes to come to terms with feminism.

2. Because of the diversity of feminist theory, I refer here to those theories identified as American feminism and French feminism. I identify American feminism as that school of thought which began as an argument for inclusion of women in the canon and verification, validation, and confirmation of women's roles, and as this inclusion progressed, American feminism began to recognize a need to talk about difference between how women operate and how men operate. I refer to French feminism as those theories particularly put forth by Hélène Cixous, Luce Irigaray, Clara Junker, and Julia Kristeva (see also Caywood and Overing; Marks and De Courtivron). While I recognize that each of these scholars approaches feminism from a different perspective—linguistic, marxist, psychoanalytic—I, like others, group them together under the heading *French feminists* out of convenience, but I am aware that even among these various subgroups there are disagreements about crucial issues.

3. For example, Flynn identifies works by Florence Howe and Maxine Hairston ("Breaking").

4. While my discussion here emphasizes *écriture féminine*, I do not mean to imply that it is the sole—or even necessarily the predominant—feminist theory that comes to composition studies. I might have just as easily explored Susan Jarratt's "feminist sophistics" or Belenky et al.'s "Women's Ways of Knowing." However, in the name of thoroughness, I concentrate on *écriture féminine* in order to succinctly identify how particular feminist theories and composition pedagogy interact.

5. De Beaugrande uses the term *feminism* in the singular to identify an all-encompassing notion of many feminisms.

6. I must point out that while both of these labels are oppressive they are not necessarily oppressive in the same way. The phrase *woman's work* seems to imply "(white) woman's work." As with the nineteenth-century white American women abolitionists who discovered their own oppression while attempting to work against slavery and announced, "We too are slaves," there is a difference in the oppression.

7. Thanks to Susan Miller for pointing me in this direction of thinking.

5. IDEOLOGY, LITERACY, AND RADICAL PEDAGOGY IN COMPOSITION STUDIES

1. In fact, discussing ideology inherently invokes particular ideologies in order to create a definition or an understanding of what *ideology* is.

2. Here I refer to the workshop entitled "Dialogic Theories and Practices in Advanced Composition" presented by Raul Sanchez, Irene Ward, Lynda Haas, and me.

3. See, for instance, Eric Havelock's *The Literate Revolution in Greece and Its Cultural Consequences* and Walter J. Ong's *Orality and Literacy: The Technologizing of the Word.*

4. In fact, Bizzell argues that much of the Hirsch bashing that was expressed in *Profession 88* and elsewhere may have been a form of careerism and politically correct bandwagoning—the same sort of careerism that many in the anti-theory camp argue against (see Chapter One).

5. Of course, this brings up a difficult dilemma regarding our ethical position of promoting values we see as right versus the position we often take as promoting ideological and cultural tolerance. I discuss this argument more thoroughly in Chapter Six.

WORKS CITED

Althusser, Louis. "Ideology and Ideological State Apparatuses." *Lenin and Philosophy and Other Essays*. Trans. Ben Brewster. London: New Left Books, 1971. 121–73.

Atkins, G. Douglas, and Michael L. Johnson, eds. *Writing and Reading Differently: Deconstruction and the Teaching of Composition and Literature*. Lawrence: University Press of Kansas, 1985.

Armstrong, Paul B. "Pluralistic Literacy." *Profession 88* (1988): 29–32.

Bakhtin, Mikhail. *Rabelais and His World*. Cambridge: MIT Press, 1968.

Barthes, Roland. *The Pleasure of the Text*. New York: Hill & Wang, 1975.

Belenky, Mary Field, et al. *Women's Ways of Knowing*. New York: Basic, 1986.

Berlin, James A. "Rhetoric and Ideology in the Writing Class." *College English* 50 (1988): 477–94.

Bizzell, Patricia. *Academic Discourse and Critical Consciousness*. Pittsburgh: University of Pittsburgh Press, 1992.

——— . Afterword. Bizzell, *Academic* 277–95.

——— . "Arguing about Literacy." Bizzell, *Academic* 238–55.

——— . "Beyond Anti-Foundationalism to Rhetorical Authority: Problems Defining 'Cultural Literacy.'" Bizzell, *Academic* 256–76.

——— . "Cognition, Convention, and Certainty: What We Need to Know about Writing." Bizzell, *Academic* 75–104.

——. "Foundationalism and Anti-Foundationalism in Composition Studies." Bizzell, *Academic* 202–21.

——. Introduction. Bizzell, *Academic* 3–30.

——. "Marxist Ideas in Composition Studies." Harkin and Schilb 52–68.

——. "Professing Literacy: A Review Essay." *Journal of Advanced Composition* 11 (1991): 315–22.

Bleich, David. Rev. of *Fragments of Rationality: Postmodernity and the Subject of Composition*, by Lester Faigley. *Journal of Advanced Composition* 14 (1994): 291–96.

Blum, Jack. "Poststructural Theories and the Postmodern Attitude in Contemporary Composition." *A Teacher's Introduction to Composition in the Rhetorical Tradition.* Edited by W. Ross Winterowd (with Jack Blum). Urbana: National Council of Teachers of English, 1994. 92–111.

Braidotti, Rosi. *Patterns of Dissonance.* New York: Routledge, 1991.

Britton, James. Foreword. *Rhetorical Traditions and the Teaching of Writing.* By C. H. Knoblauch and Lil Brannon. Upper Montclair: Boynton, 1984.

Brodkey, Linda. Afterword. *Composition Theory for the Postmodern Classroom.* Ed. Gary A. Olson and Sidney I. Dobrin. Albany: State University of New York Press, 1994. 345–47.

Bruffee, Kenneth A. "Response to the *JAC* Interview with Richard Rorty." *(Inter)views: Cross-Disciplinary Perspectives on Rhetoric and Literacy.* Ed. Gary A. Olson and Irene Gale. Carbondale: Southern Illinois University Press, 1991. 236–37.

Caywood, Cynthia L., and Gillian R. Overing, eds. *Teaching Writing: Pedagogy, Gender, and Equity.* Albany: State University of New York Press, 1986.

Cixous, Hélène. "The Laugh of the Medusa." Marks and De Courtivron 245–64.

Clifford, John. "The Subject in Discourse." Harkin and Schib 38–51.

Covino, William A. *The Art of Wondering: A Revisionist Return to the History of Rhetoric.* Portsmouth, N.H.: Boynton, 1988.

——. *Forms of Wondering: A Dialogue on Writing, for Writers.* Portsmouth, N.H.: Boynton, 1990.

Crowley, Sharon. *A Teacher's Introduction to Deconstruction.* Urbana: National Council of Teachers of English, 1989.

Culler, Jonathan. *On Deconstruction: Theory and Criticism after Structuralism.* Ithaca: Cornell University Press, 1990.

Davidson, Donald. "A Nice Derangement of Epitaphs." *Truth and Interpretation: Perspectives on the Philosophy of Donald Davidson*. Ed. Ernest lePore. Oxford: Blackwell, 1986. 433–46.

——. *Inquiries into Truth and Interpretation*. Oxford: Clarendon, 1984.

Davis, Robert Con, and Ronald Schleifer. *Contemporary Literary Criticism: Literary and Cultural Studies*. New York: Longman, 1989.

de Beaugrande, Robert. "In Search of Feminist Discourse: The 'Difficult' Case of Luce Irigaray." *College English* 50 (1988): 253–72.

de Certeau, Michel. *The Practice of Everyday Life*. Berkeley: University of California Press, 1984.

Dobrin, Sidney I. "Writing across Graduate Curriculum." *Dialogue: A Journal for Writing Specialists* 1 (1993): 65–77.

——. "Problems of Translating Dialogic Theories into Advanced Composition Pedagogy." Conference on College Composition and Communication Convention, San Diego, 3 April 1993.

Dobrin, Sidney I., and Todd Taylor. "'Radical Pedagogy': An Interview with Patricia Bizzell." *Writing On the Edge* 5 (1994): 57–68.

Elbow, Peter. *Whaxt Is English?* New York: Modern Language Assocation, 1990.

——. *Writing without Teachers*. New York: Oxford University Press, 1973.

Fish, Stanley. "Consequences." *Critical Inquiry* 11 (1985): 433–58. Rpt. in *Against Theory*. Ed. W. J. T. Mitchell. Chicago: University of Chicago Press, 1985. 106–31.

——. *Doing What Comes Naturally: Change, Rhetoric, and the Practice of Theory in Literary and Legal Studies*. Durham: Duke University Press, 1989.

Flower, Linda, et al. *Reading-to-Write: Exploring a Cognitive and Social Process*. New York: Oxford University Press, 1990.

Flynn, Elizabeth A. "Composing as a Woman." *College Composition and Communication* 39 (1988): 423–35.

Foucault, Michel. *The Archaeology of Knowledge and The Discourse on Language*. Trans. A. M. Sheridan Smith. New York: Pantheon, 1972.

——. *Discipline and Punish: The Birth of a Prison*. Trans. Alan Sheridan. New York: Vintage, 1979.

——. "The Discourse on Language." Trans. Rupert Swyr. *The Archaeology of Knowledge and The Discourse on Language*. New York: Pantheon, 1982. 215–37.

———. *The History of Sexuality, Volume I: An Introduction.* Trans. Robert Hurley, New York: Vintage, 1980.

———. *Madness and Civilization: A History of Insanity in the Age of Reason.* Trans. Richard Howard. New York: Pantheon, 1965.

———. *The Order of Things: An Archaeology of the Human Sciences.* New York: Vintage, 1966.

———. "What Is an Author?" *Language, Counter-Memory, Practice: Selected Essays and Interviews.* Ed. D. F. Bouchard. Ithaca: Cornell University Press, 1977. 113–38.

Freire, Paulo. Foreword. Kutz and Roskelly ix–x.

———. *Pedagogy of the City.* Trans. Donaldo Macedo. New York: Continuum, 1993.

———. *Pedagogy of the Oppressed.* New York: Seabury, 1970.

Gearhart, Sally Miller. "The Womanization of Rhetoric." *Women's Studies International Quarterly* 2 (1979): 195–201.

Graff, Gerald. "Vital Signs." *Voice Literary Supplement* October 1988: 23–24.

Haas-Dyson, Anne. "Confronting the Split between 'The Child' and Children: Toward New Curricular Visions of the Child Writer." *English Education* 26 (1994): 12–28.

Hairston, Maxine C. "Breaking Our Bonds and Reaffirming Our Connections." *College Composition and Communication* 36 (1985): 272–82.

———. "Comment and Response." *College English* 52 (1990): 694–96.

Hall, Stuart. "The Rediscovery of 'Ideology': The Return of the 'Repressed' in Media Studies." *Culture, Society, and the Media.* Ed. Michael Gurevitch et al. London: Methuen, 1982. 56–90.

Haraway, Donna. "Situated Knowledges: The Science Question in Feminism and the Privilege of Partial Perspectives." *Simians, Cyborgs, and Women: The Reinvention of Nature.* New York: Routledge, 1991. 183–201.

Harkin, Patricia. "The Postdisciplinary Politics of Lore." Harkin and Schilb 124–38.

Harkin, Patricia, and John Schilb, eds. *Contending with Words: Composition and Rhetoric in a Postmodern Age.* New York: Modern Language Association, 1991.

———. Introduction. Harkin and Schilb 1–10.

Harned, Jon. "Post-structuralism and the Teaching of Composition." *Freshman English News* 15.2 (1986): 10–16.

Harris, Joseph. "The Rhetoric of Theory." *Writing Theory and Critical Theory.* Ed. John Clifford and John Schilb. New York: Modern Language Association, 1994. 141–47.

Hatlen, Burton. "Michel Foucault and the Discourse[s] of English." *College English* 50 (1988): 786–801.

Havelock, Eric. *The Literate Revolution in Greece and Its Cultural Consequences.* Princeton: Princeton University Press, 1982.

Herzberg, Bruce. "Michel Foucault's Rhetorical Theory." Harkin and Schilb 69–81.

Hiller, Janet, and Barbara Osburg. "A Comment on 'Lacan, Transferences, and Writing Instruction.'" *College English* 50 (1988): 819–20.

Hinchey, Pat. "Lost in Translation: Perils on the Uncertain Route from Reform Theory to Practice." *Council Chronicle* 3.4 (1994): 20, 6–7.

Hirsch, E. D., Jr. "Cultural Literacy." *American Scholar* 52 (1982–83): 159–69.

———. "Cultural Literacy." *Journal of Basic Writing* 3 (1980): 27–47.

———. *Cultural Literacy: What Every American Needs to Know.* Boston: Houghton, 1987.

———. *The Philosophy of Composition.* Chicago: University of Chicago Press, 1977.

Hourigan, Maureen M. *Literacy as Social Exchange: Intersections of Class, Gender, and Culture.* Albany: State University of New York Press, 1994.

Howe, Florence. "Identity and Expression: A Writing Course for Women." *College English* 32 (1971): 863–71.

Irigaray, Luce. *Speculum of the Other Woman.* Ithaca: Cornell University Press, 1985.

———. *This Sex Is Not One.* Ithaca: Cornell University Press, 1985.

Jarratt, Susan. "Feminism and Composition: The Case for Conflict." Harkin and Schilb 105–23.

———. *Rereading the Sophisis: Classical Rhetoric Refigured.* Carbondale: Southern Illinois University Press, 1991.

Johnson, Barbara. *The Critical Difference: Essays in the Contemporary Rhetoric of Reading.* Baltimore: Johns Hopkins University Press, 1980.

Junker, Clara. "Writing (with) Cixous." *College English* 50 (1988): 424–36.

———. "Clara Junker Responds." *College English* 50 (1988): 825–27.

Kent, Thomas. "Beyond System: The Rhetoric of Paralogy." *College English* 51 (1989): 492–507.

——— . "Interpretation and Triangulation: A Davidsonian Critique of Reader-Oriented Literary Theory." *Literary Theory after Davidson.* Ed. Reed Way Dasenbrock. University Park: Pennsylvania State University Press, 1993.

——— . "Language Philosophy, Writing, and Reading: A Conversation with Donald Davidson." *Journal of Advanced Composition* 13 (1993): 1–20.

——— . "On the Very Idea of a Discourse Community." *College Composition and Communication* 42 (1991): 425–45.

——— . "Paralogic Hermeneutics and the Possibilites of Rhetoric." *Rhetoric Review* 8 (1989): 24–42.

Knapp, Steven, and Walter Benn Michaels. "Against Theory." *Against Theory.* Ed. W. J. T. Mitchell. Chicago: University of Chicago Press, 1985.

Knoblauch, C. H., and Lil Brannon. *Rhetorical Traditions and the Teaching of Writing.* Upper Montclair: Boynton, 1984.

Kogan, Steve. "A Comment on *College English.*" *College English* 52 (1990): 473–74.

Kutz, Eleanor, and Hephzibah Roskelly. *An Unquiet Pedagogy: Transforming Practice in the English Classroom.* Portsmouth, N.H.: Boynton, 1991.

Larson, Gary. "The Far Side." Cartoon. *The Far Side Calendar* 30 March 1988.

——— . "The Far Side." Cartoon. *The Far Side Calendar* 23 March 1992.

LeFevre, Karen Burke. *Invention as a Social Act.* Carbondale: Southern Illinois University Press, 1987.

Lunsford, Andrea A., Helene Moglen, and James Slevin, eds. *The Right to Literacy.* New York: Modern Language Association, 1990.

Lyotard, Jean François. *The Postmodern Condition: A Report on Knowledge.* Trans. Geoff Bennington and Brian Massumi. Minneapolis: University of Minnesota Press, 1984.

Mailloux, Stephen. *Rhetorical Power.* Ithaca: Cornell University Press, 1989.

Marks, Elaine, and Isabelle De Courtivron, eds. *New French Feminisms.* Brighton: Harvester, 1981. 245–64.

Miller, Susan. "The Feminization of Composition." *The Politics of Writing Instruction: Postsecondary.* Ed. Richard Bullock and John Trimbur. Portsmouth: Boynton, 1991. 39–53.

——— . *Textual Carnivals: The Politics of Composition.* Carbondale: Southern Illinois University Press, 1991.

Moglen, Helene. "Allan Bloom and E. D. Hirsch: Educational Reform as Tragedy and Farce." *Profession 88* (1988): 59–64.

Morley, David. *Family Television: Cultural Power and Domestic Leisure.* London: Commedia, 1986.

Neel, Jasper. *Plato, Derrida, and Writing.* Carbondale: Southern Illinois University Press, 1988.

Noack, Paul. "Crisis instead of Revolution: On the Instrumental Change of Social Innovation." *Innovation/Renovation: New Perspectives on the Humanities.* Ed. Ihab Hassan and Sally Hassan. Madison: University of Wisconsin Press, 1983. 65–84.

North, Stephen M. *The Making of Knowledge in Composition: Portrait of an Emerging Field.* Upper Montclair: Boynton, 1987.

Odell, Lee. *Theory and Practice in the Teaching of Writing: Rethinking the Discipline.* Carbondale: Southern Illinois University Press, 1993.

Ohmann, Richard. *Politics of Letters.* Middletown, Conn.: Wesleyan University Press, 1987.

Olson, Gary A. "Literary Theory, Philosophy of Science, and Persuasive Discourse: Thoughts from a Neo-premodernist." *Journal of Advanced Composition* 13 (1993): 283–309.

―――. "On Leaving *JAC.*" *Journal of Advanced Composition* 14 (1994): v–viii.

―――. "The Role of Theory in Composition Scholarship." *Freshman English News* 19 (1991): 4–5.

―――. "Social Construction and Composition Theory: A Conversation with Richard Rorty." *(Inter)views: Cross-Disciplinary Perspectives on Rhetoric and Literacy.* Ed. Gary A. Olson and Irene Gale. Carbondale: Southern Illinois University Press, 1991. 227–35.

Ong, Walter J. *Orality and Literacy: The Technologizing of the Word.* New York: Methuen, 1982.

Phelps, Louise Whetherbee. *Composition as a Human Science: Contributions to the Self-Understanding of a Discipline.* Oxford: Oxford University Press, 1988.

―――. "Practical Wisdom and the Geography of Knowledge in Composition." *College English* 53 (1991): 863–85.

Raines, Howell. *Fly Fishing through the Midlife Crisis.* New York: Anchor, 1993.

Raschke, Debrah. "A Comment on 'Writing (with) Cixous.'" *College English* 50 (1988): 822–25.

Ray, Ruth E. *The Practice of Theory: Teacher Research in Composition.* Urbana: National Council of Teachers of English, 1993.

Raymond, James C. "Aftershocks of Theory: A Rhetoric of Relationships in Current Composition Journals." *Focuses* 6 (1993): 86–92.

Ritchie, Joy S. "Confronting the 'Essential' Problem: Reconnecting Feminist Theory and Pedagogy." *Journal of Advanced Composition.* 10 (1990): 249–73.

Rorty, Richard. *Contingency, Irony, and Solidarity.* New York: Cambridge University Press, 1989. 3–22.

———. *Philosophy and the Mirror of Nature.* Princeton: Princeton University Press, 1979.

Said, Edward. *The World, the Text, and the Critic.* Cambridge: Harvard University Press, 1983.

Sanchez, Raul. "David Bleich and the Politics of Anti-Intellectualism: A Response." *Journal of Advanced Composition* 14 (1994): 579–81.

———. "Dialogue and Post-Process Theory in Advanced Composition." Conference on College Composition and Communication Convention, San Diego, 3 April 1993.

Schilb, John. "Composition and Poststructuralism: A Tale of Two Conferences." *College Composition and Communication* 40 (1989): 422–43.

———. "Cultural Studies, Postmodernism, and Composition." Harkin and Schilb 173–88.

———. "What's at Stake in the Conflict between 'Theory' and 'Practice' in Composition?" *Rhetoric Review* 10 (1991): 91–97.

Sheils, Merrill. "Why Jonny Can't Write." *Newsweek* 8 December 1975: 58–65.

Shepard, Jean. "Two Comments on *College English.*" *College English* 49 (1987): 933–35.

Shor, Ira. *Critical Teaching and Everyday Life.* Chicago: University of Chicago Press, 1987.

———. ed. *Freire for the Classroom: A Sourcebook for Liberatory Teaching.* Portsmouth, N.H.: Boynton, 1987.

Shor, Ira, and Paulo Freire. *A Pedagogy for Liberation.* South Hadley, Mass.: Bergin, 1987.

Sipiora, Phillip, and Janet Atwill. "Rhetoric and Cultural Explanation: A Discussion with Gayatri Chakravorty Spivak." *(Inter)views: Cross-Disciplinary Perspectives on Rhetoric and Literacy.* Ed. Gary A. Olson and Irene Gale. Carbondale: Southern Illinois University Press, 1991. 243–54.

Sledd, Andrew, and James Sledd. "Hirsch's Use of His Sources in *Cultural Literacy*: A Critique." *Profession 88* (1988): 33–39.

Smit, David W. "Hall of Mirrors: Antifoundationalist Theory and the Teaching of Writing." *JAC: A Journal of Composition Theory* 15 (1994): 35–52.

Snyder, Carol. "Analyzing Classifications: Foucault for Advanced Writing." *College Composition and Communication* 25 (1984): 209–16.

Sosnoski, James J. "Postmodern Teachers in Their Postmodern Classrooms: Socrates Begone!" Harkin and Schilb 198–219.

Sowell, Thomas. "The Fall of the Ivory Tower: Money and the Moral Bankruptcy of Colleges." Editorial. *The Atlanta Journal and Constitution* 7 June 1994, sec. A: 8.

Spellmeyer, Kurt. "Foucault and the Freshman Writer: Considering the Self in Discourse." *College English* 51 (1989): 715–29.

Stygall, Gail. "Resisting Privilege: Basic Writing and Foucault's Author Function." *College Composition and Communication* 45 (1994): 320–41.

Sullivan, Mary Margaret. "Two Comments on Maxine Hairston's Letter." *College English* 53 (1991): 477–78.

Tompkins, Jane. "A Short Course in Post-Structuralism." *College English* 50 (1988): 733–47.

Trimbur, John. "John Trimbur Responds." *College English* 52 (1990): 696–700.

Trimbur, John, and Mara Holt. "Richard Rorty: Philosophy without Foundations." *The Philosophy of Discourse: The Rhetorical Turn in Twentieth-Century Thought*. Vol. 1. Ed. Chip Sills and George H. Jensen. Portsmouth, N.H.: Boynton, 1992. 70–94.

Ulmer, Gregory. *Applied Grammatology: Post(e)-Pedagogy from Jacques Derrida to Joseph Beuys*. Baltimore: Johns Hopkins University Press, 1985.

Vitanza, Victor J. "Three Countertheses: Or, A Critical In(ter)vention into Composition Theories and Pedagogies." Harkin and Schilb 139–72.

Ward, Irene. *Literacy, Ideology, and Dialogue: Towards a Dialogic Pedagogy*. Albany: State University of New York Press, 1994.

Warnock, John. "Cultural Literacy: A Worm in the Bud?" *ADE Bulletin* (1982): 1–7.

Watterson, Bill. "Calvin and Hobbes." Cartoon. *The Tampa Tribune* 11 February 1993.

Will, George. "Literary Politics." *Newsweek* 22 April 1991. 72.

———. "Trendy Theories and Illiterate Kids." *Tampa Tribune* 2 July 1995. A8.

Worsham, Lynn. "Writing against Writing: The Predicament of *Ecriture Féminine* in Composition." Harkin and Schilb 82–104.

INDEX